Grow

C

GROW!

Knofel Staton

Illustrated by James Seward

A division of Standard Publishing
Cincinnati, Ohio
39999

DEDICATED

to the one person

whose prayers have followed me all of my life:

my mother, ETHEL SCHOFIELD

Library of Congress Catalog Card No. 77-082120
ISBN: 0-87239-177-9

© 1977
The STANDARD PUBLISHING COMPANY, Cincinnati, Ohio.
Division of STANDEX INTERNATIONAL CORPORATION.
Printed in U.S.A.

Preface

From one man (Jesus) to twelve, to three thousand, to a number no man could count: that is the history of the growth of Christianity within the first thirty-five years after Jesus was born. How did God do it? Not with gimmicks or tricks, but through Jesus and His followers, through the power of changed lives.

What kind of followers did Jesus have? Supermen and Wonderwomen? We think the church would grow in the same way today, if the same kind of people were around?

Well, we do have the same kind of people around today. You won't read about any Supermen or Wonderwomen in the New Testament. You will read about people who are very much like the school janitor, the meter-reader, the grocery store clerk, and others with whom you are familiar. They were the kind of people who were responsible for the growth of the church.

Somewhere in this book you will see yourself. You may find a little bit of yourself in many of those people studied. You probably will be able to see the members of your church portrayed in some of these characters. In all of these people, you will find an example to follow.

All of these people had three things in common: a trust in Jesus, the need to grow, and the desire to grow. In these ways, I hope, they are no different from us. I hope that, after reading this book, you will be challenged and ready to shout, "I am going to grow up!"

NOTE: Some of the characteristics discussed for each personality are not expressly stated in the Scripture, but are inferred as I immersed myself in the passages that spoke of the person and in the writings of the person. Such words as "suspect," "guess," "probably," "may have," "perhaps," "possibly," "imagine," "must have," "evidently," etc., will help you to determine when such inferences were made.

Unless otherwise identified, every Scripture quotation is from The New American Standard Bible, © The Lockman Foundation 1960, 1962, 1963, 1968, 1971, 1972, 1973, 1975, and are used by permission. Those Scriptures marked with an asterisk (*) are my own loose paraphrases.

APPRECIATION

Because I feel that it is not entirely correct for an author to receive all the credit for his book, I should like to express appreciation to the following:

My wife, Julia, copy editor and typist.

Phyllis Sanders and Jacqueline Westers, the editors who contributed toward the readability of the text and prepared the manuscript for printing.

Frank Sutton and James Seward, who prepared the art.

—*Knofel Staton*

Contents

Born To Grow

Every day she changes. It is amazing how we can actually see her mind and body develop from day to day. Watching a baby grow is one of the most exciting experiences in life!

Rachel, our youngest daughter, is less than a year old. She is not as mature as her older brother and sisters, but we do not expect her to be. One thing is certain, however; she is on her way. We don't expect her to think and act and react exactly the same as our other children, but we do expect her to grow and progress.

It would be heartbreaking if Rachel stayed at her present level of development the rest of her life. We expect her to walk, to run, and to jump. We hope to watch her climb stairs and later climb trees. We listen to her coo and babble now, but we expect her to soon say "ma-ma" and "da-da"; then we hope she will say "Mother" and "Father." Perhaps in the far future she will be able to say "Knofel," although she will never be old enough to understand why my mother named me that. Now we are coaxing Rachel to make sounds with her mouth, but one of these days we won't be able to shut her up.

Rachel is crawling now, emptying wastebaskets and cabinets. Soon she will walk, run, and climb. Someday she will be walking down the aisle in her bridal gown. It will happen much more quickly than we can imagine. We will say, "Oh, no, not so soon!" She will say, "Ah, yes, at last!"

Rachel's mother, Julia, gets up with Rachel in the

middle of the night. It won't be long before Julia will be getting up in the middle of the night with a grand-baby while the new mother, Rachel, recuperates from the birth of her child. Rachel, who dirties her diapers now, will soon be washing the diapers of her own children.

What fantastic changes take place in a person's life! How exciting to watch and to be involved in a growing, changing life! How the years rush by amidst such excitement!

A Growing Spiritual Life

Our physical lives are begun in order to grow and change, and we delight in it. Our spiritual lives also are begun to grow and change.

As we are physically born, we must also be spiritually born in order to develop according to God's design for us. As physical birth is necessary in order to express and enjoy temporary life, so spiritual birth is necessary to demonstrate and delight in eternal life. That is why Jesus came, that we might have life abundantly (John 10:10).

Jesus did not come to suppress our progress, but He came to enable us to progress and develop. Many people think that Jesus is like some fuddy-duddy in the sky who likes to spoil our parties or fun. They think that He squelches what it means to be human. They equate being human to "eating, drinking, and being merry." It is only human, they say, to go from party to party, from drink to drink, from drug to drug, and from bed to bed. But that is not being human; it is being subhuman.

Jesus came to demonstrate to us how to be truly human, how to develop and progress as individuals. It was after He came that early Christians, viewing His life, said, "Don't let the world squeeze you into its mold; let God remold you from within" (Romans 12:2)* When that remolding begins, a new birth takes place, a new creature is fashioned.

8

The New Birth

Two births are necessary for a person to really progress as a person. That is why Jesus said, "You must be born again" (John 3:7). The word "again" also means "from above." Jesus meant we must be born from above as well as from below. He was saying that we must be born of God (1 John 3:9; 4:7; 5:1, 4, 18). We are to have a heavenly Father as well as an earthly father.

We can have it both ways! Fantastic! We can be adopted by God (Romans 8:15), become joint-heirs with Jesus, and be born of God. What a beautiful thought!

Both the adoption by God and the new birth make clear to us our worth, our natures, and our potential. To be adopted spotlights the fact that we were planned for and wanted. We were *chosen;* we are not the result of an accident. "He chose us in Him before the foundation of the world" (Ephesians 1:4). Now, that is being wanted for a *long* time. Can you imagine anyone wanting you from that far back? What a loving Father!

Being joint-heirs with Jesus means we have *worth.* In God's family we have an equal inheritance with Jesus. What a mind-boggling truth! God does not consider us nobodies; He considers us somebodies of great worth and adopts us into His body, or family.

We are not only adopted; we are also born of God. God actually puts His seed in us. John wrote that His seed "abides" in us (1 John 3:9). "Seed" is the Greek word *sperma,* from which comes our word "sperm." God puts His own nature in us. We are in all reality God's children because of our new birth (3:2).

The "seed" that God puts within us is His own Spirit (3:24). Long ago, He chose to both adopt us and to beget us by His Spirit. We are born again, then, when our response meets God's initiative. When our faith and obedience meet God's gift in Jesus, our new birth takes place.

Potential For Growth

At the time of our new birth, we can joyously pray, "I thank You, God, that I am not the person I was; nor am I the person I will become." Growth should follow birth. Peter wrote, "like newborn babes, long for the pure milk of the word, that by it you may grow" (1 Peter 2:2). We are born to grow.

What are we to become? What is to be our aim? What is to be the target to hit? God has a target in mind. He wants us to become like Him and/or like Jesus. He wants each of us to grow, change, and develop until our character, actions, and reactions are like His. We will then reflect the true image of our Father. We will then treat each other as the Father wants us to treat His other sons and daughters. We will then treat His whole creation the way He wants us to take care of His property.

We parents have goals in mind that we hope our children will reach. We want them to be loving, moral, and responsible. We want them to be happy and healthy. We have the type of success in mind that we would like them to achieve. We cannot *force* them to reach those goals, for they have minds of their own and will make their own way. Instead, we seek to guide and instruct them, so their decisions will lead them to the goals we wish for them, without their losing their individualities.

The heavenly Father is the same way with us. He wants us all to have the same kind of character that Jesus has, but He allows us our uniqueness as individuals. I can be myself and still become like Jesus. You can be yourself and still become like Jesus. His goal for us is that all of our differences in personality, aptitude, and interests can be channeled into the image of Jesus. We can become tools in the hands of the Almighty Creator. We are different, but we can permit the character of Jesus to shine through us.

We are to change and grow each day and become more like Jesus. That is our target, our aim.

This is not an impossible or unreachable goal. We can attain it because we have His Spirit within us. We have God's nature within us. God has designed this target, and He has made it within our reach. To help us to achieve this goal, He has outlined the target for us clearly in the Scriptures:

(1) "Therefore you are to be perfect, as your heavenly Father is perfect" (Matthew 5:48). This word "perfect" means "mature." It means reaching the required goal. The foregoing verses (43-47) tell us that the goal includes loving the way God loves (without prejudice).

(2) We are "to attain . . . to a mature man" (Ephesians 4:13). The word for "mature" is the same word used in Matthew 5:48. It means coming to a unity of belief and knowledge of Christ, and reaching "the measure of the stature which belongs to the fulness of Christ" (Ephesians 4:13). This goal includes not being carried away by every fad that comes along (Ephesians 4:14), speaking the truth in love (v. 15), and not having hard hearts and lazy minds (v. 18).

(3) We are to "put on the new self," which is in the likeness of God (4:24). We are to start a new life. We are to become new persons. We are to put away our old life-styles and our bad habits.

We begin this new life as spiritual babies. As babies we are full of selfishness and jealousies, but we must never stay that way. We do not want our children to remain as babies, physically or mentally. We want them to grow and change. God certainly does not want His children to remain as babies spiritually. He wants us to grow continuously toward the target.

Hitting The Target

In order to hit the target, we must be dissatisfied. We must not be content to stay on one level of spiritual development. Paul put it this way: "I press on toward the goal for the prize of the upward call of God in Christ Jesus" (Philippians 3:14).

We also must be committed to change. Without this commitment, dissatisfaction would lead us to despair and defeat. We must be determined to take good aim at God's target and know that we can hit it.

Growth is also caused by God whose Spirit is at work within us. Our involvement in His Word, His work, and His church allows Him to change us daily. Our involvement with each other is for the express purpose of helping each other become like Jesus. No one is very much like Jesus at the time of his new birth. We need the help of each other, just as a new baby needs help when he is born into a physical family.

Being a growing Christian is a thrilling and exciting adventure. We are to grow and change each day. Let us consider the lives of others who can be examples to us as we aim for God's target.

Overview Of The Book

In this book we are going to study several people who aimed to reach God's target. They were very much like you and me. They were spiritual babies for a while. They had their spiritual hang-ups and problems. They experienced growing pains. It will be exciting for us to note their progress.

It is my hope that you will not only notice the growth in the spiritual lives of these people, but that you will also see Jesus, for it is He who made it all possible. He is both the Alpha and Omega of our new lives. He is the beginning and He is the goal, the author and the finisher of our faith (Hebrews 12:2).

This fascinating adventure of studying the spiritual growth of individuals is much like the adventure of watching our children grow into adulthood. As we pursue this adventure, let us realize that we all can grow spiritually (yes, even today!) and become like Jesus. God has not outlined the target that He desires for us to hit and then moved it beyond our capabilities. We only need to ask ourselves if we are aiming for the right target!

Only a Teenager

If both my wife and I were killed in an accident, what would happen to our children? With whom would the court place them? We were concerned about the answers to these questions a short time ago, so we decided to do something about it. We chose a couple whom we believed best to rear and take care of our children, and then made it legal.

Whom should we choose? We wanted people who shared our commitment to Christ and His church. We wanted a couple who valued people above property. We felt the couple should have had experience in rearing children. We did not want our children to be their first-time experiments.

What if you had this decision to make? Whom would you choose? Would you want the people to have the financial means to send your children to college and promise to do so? Would you want them to be in their twenties or thirties? Would you want them to be settled and secure in their home and career? Would you want them to be apartment dwellers, renters, or homeowners?

Would you consider an engaged couple who might get custody of your children before they were married? Would you choose a couple who would grow up with your children, fine young teenagers, for example? Would you *dare* to choose a couple of teens not yet married?

God had to make a similar decision when He chose guardian parents to have custody of His Son. Did He choose a wealthy couple who could give His

13

Mary

Son every advantage? Did He choose a middle-class, secure, and homey couple? No! He chose two poverty-stricken young people out of the youth group of the synagogue in Nazareth. They were engaged to each other, but not yet married. What a couple for God to choose to rear His Son!

In that day, Jewish girls were engaged as young as nine to eleven years of age, while the boys were usually about seventeen or eighteen. They were to be engaged for one year before marriage. Mary could have been under twelve years old when the angel appeared to her, and Joseph about eighteen. If Mary was eleven, say, when she was engaged, she would have been almost twelve when the angel appeared to her, and thirteen when Jesus was born.

What a young woman she was! Yet she was a model for all womanhood. It is true that some religious groups have elevated her too highly, but it is also possible that others have ignored the person God chose to become the earthly mother of His Son. While her Son is to be worshiped and not she, at least she should be honored. Whom God has favored (Luke 1:28), we have no right to disfavor.

Faithful

Of course, Mary was frightened when the angel came and spoke to her (Luke 1:28-30), and her fear soon turned to bewilderment. "I'm going to have a baby? How can this be?" (1:34)* She was a virgin, and was perplexed as to how this could happen.

Even after the angel told her, Mary could not possibly have understood how it was to happen. After all, how can you explain how the Holy Spirit could cause a virgin to get pregnant? She did not understand. All she could do was trust the words, "Nothing will be impossible with God" (1:37).

Something is wrong with our faith when we must have all the whys, hows, and results outlined in black and white before we obey God. On this point, Mary is not only a model for all womanhood, but for all mankind. The angel did not even hint to her as to how her condition would affect her relationship with her parents, or how her friends in the youth group in the synagogue would react. After all, a pregnant, unmarried girl would not be well thought of!

What would happen to her reputation? Yet, that would not be the major question. What would become of her *life?* Whenever an engaged girl committed infidelity against her fiance, she could be stoned to death!

How would this affect her relationship with Joseph and their plans for marriage? Do you think for one minute that Joseph would buy this line: "Honey, I've got good news and bad news. I'm going to have a baby boy who won't even be named after you. But don't get upset. I'm still a virgin. The Holy Spirit has made me pregnant"? Who could believe such a story, even from the girl he loved?

Joseph decided to call it quits. He cared too much for Mary to make the assumed infidelity public, so he decided to divorce her quietly (Matthew 1:19). At that time an engaged couple was legally bound to each other. The only way to break the engagement was through a divorce proceeding. Mary would become an unwed mother, and she would be disgraced.

Yet, with all these potentialities ahead of her—alienation at home, excommunication from the synagogue, a broken engagement, a ruined reputation—Mary said to the angel, "Behold, the bondslave of the Lord; be it done to me according to your word" (Luke 1:38). What a model for us!

God always honors a faith like Mary's. It was like Abraham's faith. He left home not knowing where he was going, only knowing that God said to go (Hebrews 11:8). Mary did not know what would happen to her, but she knew that God could do the impossible, and make all things happen for the good (Romans 8:28).

Without such a faith, it is impossible to please God (Hebrews 11:6). It is not correct to make our decisions upon our intellectual, common sense, or experience-oriented conclusions when we have a "thus saith the Lord" (an expressed command) staring us in the face.

God lovingly helped Mary. He stopped Joseph in his plans to put her away. The angel told him all about the child Mary was carrying (Matthew 1:19-21), and told him to marry her.

How do you suppose Mary felt in her wedding gown, very evidently pregnant? In those days, wedding dates could not be moved up. What would her relatives say amongst themselves while publicly wishing them well? How could Mary expect Joseph to accept some of the consequences, such as a marriage that could not be consummated until after the baby was born? Joseph was a great and compassionate husband for her!

Submissive Servant

Mary was indeed an individual, as was evident in her making her own decision. She was willing to decide to obey God, in spite of all the pressures to do otherwise. Yet she did not live for her individuality. She knew what it would mean to submit, both to God and to her husband.

Mary's body was changing. She was living at home and preparing for that firstborn child. She had plenty of problems of her own, but she decided to visit her relative, Elizabeth, remembering that she was also pregnant. Elizabeth was much older, and perhaps without help at home (if Zacharias was the typical husband). It may have been that Mary also felt the need of advice and encouragement of an older woman in similar circumstances. But if Elizabeth needed help during her last months of pregnancy, and it was likely, she could not have had a better choice.

Mary had the right to demand attention and spe-

17

cial treatment for herself, but instead she was willing to give attention and special treatment to another. She lived for others! What a model for us to follow! No wonder God chose her to be the mother of Him who would give His life for others. Jesus' own unselfishness was strengthened because He could observe the attitude of His mother toward others.

Now it is the last month of Mary's pregnancy. She is terribly uncomfortable. Joseph has had a brainstorm, "I want you to go with me to Bethlehem for the census." Doesn't he understand how miserable she is? She can barely make it to the rooftop or down the street to the market, let alone ride a donkey from Nazareth to Bethlehem! "You've got to be kidding!" But no, he is not kidding.

It was not required that the woman travel to the city of her ancestry for the census, only the man. Why did Joseph decide to take Mary? Perhaps he was afraid she would have the baby without him. Perhaps he felt she would be safer and happier with him. Many people still believed she had been unfaithful. Perhaps he knew the Scripture that said the Savior was to be born in Bethlehem; or perhaps God gave him special guidance.

Whatever the reasons for Joseph's decision, Mary submitted and agreed to go with him. One who has not experienced the last few months of a pregnancy cannot fully appreciate the submissiveness of Mary to consent to ride a donkey for three days over rough terrain.

Joseph probably traveled much like many men today. He decided at the beginning of the day how far he wanted to go before stopping for the night. No matter what happened, he felt he would be a failure if he didn't achieve that goal. I can hear Mary saying to Joseph in the late afternoon, "Dear, why don't we stop at this nice grassy spot for the night?" But Joseph probably replied, "Oh, I think we can make it to Bethlehem tonight. We have lots of daylight left." So

18

on they went, Into Bethlehem they came, very late, and with no reservations at the inn. But Mary did not complain.

After the baby was born, they got a house and began to settle down. That donkey trip was enough for a while. Joseph got a carpenter's job, and so their life seemed secure. Two years, or almost, had passed (Matthew 2:16), with no help from either mother or mother-in-law. Still Mary did not complain. Jesus was walking and beginning to talk, and yet there had been no trips to see the grandparents.

The two young people were still away from home with their first baby. What next? A shocker! Another long trip, but not back home. It was to be a trip to a foreign country—Egypt. Yet Mary submitted. Others could question how her Son could be the Messiah for the Jews and be from Egypt, but Mary maintained the attitudes she had from the beginning: "I am Your bond-servant" and "God can do the impossible."

What attitudes for Jesus to live with and to observe! Many times Jesus was to face terrible complications for doing things God's way, but His mother would teach Him by her example how He should live.

What about our children? What kind of attitudes are we modeling for them, that will help them through tough situations when they are thirty years old? The kind of man Jesus was cannot be divorced from the kind of boyhood He experienced.

Honored, But Not Arrogant

Few of Mary's personality traits shine through more clearly than her humility. She had every reason, from the human viewpoint, to be full of pride. She had every right to demand special attention and treatment. Just consider what was said to her:

(1) An angel of the Lord said, "Hail, favored one!" (Luke 1:28).

(2) Elizabeth said, "Blessed among women are you, and blessed is the fruit of your womb! . . . the

19

mother of my Lord . . . when the sound of your greeting reached my ears, the baby leaped in my womb for joy" (1:42-44).

(3) The shepherds told her what had happened to them and what the angels told them, "A Savior, who is Christ the Lord" is born (2:11-17).

•(4) Simeon declared that in her Son is the world's salvation (2:26-32).

(5) The Wise-men came to worship and give gifts (Matthew 2:11).

God's special guidance had been showered upon that family through angels, dreams, prophecies, visions, a guiding star, and physical protection from Herod's madness. What was done and said would have been enough to make anyone arrogant. Mary treasured all that she heard and pondered in amazement (Luke 2:1ke 2:19, 33), but she never allowed any of it to make her prideful.

Mary never bragged about how God performed miracles around her. She never drew a crowd around her to relate her experiences to people and have them follow her. She never set out to make a name for herself. She did not travel to make speeches or become popular. She did not request VIP room in the hospital because of who she was. The farm animals' living quarters were good enough. The trough for the hay was good enough for her Son's first bed. She did not need everything beautiful and new for the baby. Her priorities were so different from what they could have been.

Even after the resurrection, Mary met with the others as one of them, not as one who should be in the spotlight (Acts 1:14). After Judas died, she didn't demand that the next apostle chosen be a woman who knew Jesus better than any of them. She never lost the attitude of being an undemanding servant.

We do not hear about Mary after Acts 1:14, but that is to her credit. She was great because she was unselfish. She brought the Messiah into the world and reared Him, but in no way would she ever over-shadow Him. She was a fulfilled woman.

What an example she was to the King of kings! He could have demanded His rights many times, but He didn't. Instead He emptied himself of all rights, the essence of humility (Philippians 2:5-11). I'm sure He learned something about humility at home.

A Good Mother

It would be difficult not to show some favoritism toward a gifted child, but there is no hint that Mary did so. She had many other children (Matthew 13:55; Mark 6:3), but she did not coerce them to treat Jesus differently. In fact, Jesus' brothers did not believe in Him. They tried to prod Him to show His hand (John 7:3-5), and their mother did not interfere. She joined His brothers when they came to take Him home (Mark 3:31, 32). The whole family was concerned because people were saying He had lost His mind (3:21).

Although Mary was a concerned mother, she was not dominating. She did not try to control her Son's life when He was mature. She permitted Him to be on His own without interfering. She cut the apron strings. She did not try to stop Him when He left home to travel and preach. She did not try to talk Him into getting married, even though He was thirty.

She did not say that His statement that He had no place to lay His head was embarrassing to the family. She did not argue when He did not carry out her wishes at the wedding feast (John 2:4, 5). She did not stand between Him and the soldiers in the garden to prevent His arrest. He had a mission to accomplish; she did not try to detour it.

What a mother! Do you think it was easy for her to hear her neighbors say that her Son was crazy (Mark 3:21)? Surely she was not able to stifle the sobs when the hometown church tried to kill Him after His first sermon (Luke 4:16-30). How do you think she felt when He would not come home with her, and declared that His family included those who did God's will (Mark 3:34, 35)?

Didn't she suffer agonies that only a parent could when her Son hung for hours on the cruel cross! She could not close her ears to the jeers and slanderous words. Her eyes beheld His naked body, bruised, bleeding, and dying. Don't you imagine she wondered how God could allow this to happen to His Son? Oh, Mary, how tough it must have been for you!

Then, after the resurrection, she could expect her Son to spend some time with her, but He spent most of His time with others. Only a mother could understand the pain she must have experienced.

Mary mothered Jesus, but did not smother Him. She did not run Him when He became a man. It was not easy for her to let Him go, but it was necessary. How many mothers today can let their children go and grow as adults? How many boys are discouraged from being preachers because Mom can't bear to have them leave home, to have an unaccredited Bible College education, to live in a parsonage, to have a meager salary, or to go to a faraway mission field?

Jesus was free to serve God, partly because of a fantastic mother. God certainly made a wise choise. Mary held on to Jesus when she should have, and let go when she should have. She faced many tough decisions. When she was unmarried and no one understood her, she made the right decision. When her Son was ridiculed and misunderstood, she still did the right thing.

At the beginning of Jesus' advent, we see Mary singing a song (Luke 1:46-55). At the church's advent we see her in prayer (Acts 1:14). The Christ was born amid the singing of Mary; the church was born amid the praying of Mary. Her attitudes of faith, humility, submission, and service never diminished. Is it any wonder that Jesus had such a high regard for womanhood? Her example of womanhood and motherhood will live on for eternity!

The Oddity

What an odd-looking duck! He looked more like a wild animal than a man, with all that camel's hair wrapped around him and tied with leather strips. Do you think he would sit down to eat a regular meal? Not on your life! When he got hungry, he would go out in the fields and catch some grasshoppers, and stick his hand into a hole in a tree or a rock to pull out some honey. He would roast the locusts and pop them into his mouth as if he were eating Planter's Peanuts. He was thirty years old, old enough to know better, old enough to be married. But what woman in her right mind would want *him?*

What if he tried to come to our church? Heaven forbid! It is hard enough trying to get our teenagers to dress up for the services, without having an adult like that for an example! Let him address the congregation looking like that? Never! He would drive away visitors and embarrass the regulars.

If we are perfectly honest with ourselves, we know that we probably would not invite such a man to our worship services. We couldn't make the excuse that we did not know he was around. Anyone who was that different from other folk would be well known in the community. After all, he spent most of his time in the country, not even living in a cabin. He lived out in the open, in caves, on the ground, or in some makeshift shelter.

What would happen if he *did* attend our services? How would we treat such a man in our church, especially if he didn't make a move to change his eating

23

habits, his sleeping place, or his clothes? Would his inner character of strict morality and dedication to God matter to us? Unless he tried to eat, sleep, and dress as we do, would we elect him to be our Sunday-school teacher? Would we cringe if he helped serve Communion? Maybe others like him would start coming. He could destroy the church!

Wait a minute! What about the Scripture verse that says, "Do not neglect to show hospitality to strangers, for by this some have entertained angels without knowing it" (Hebrews 13:2)? Can we forget that one? Let us not be too quick to decide whom God will or will not use. God does not judge by a person's appearance, but by his heart (John 7:24). It was just such a country hermit, thought to be strange and weird by the people of his time, who was the forerunner of Christ and the church.

I imagine if we were in charge of choosing people to launch the church, our choices would be quite different from God's choices. He did not choose many from the nobility. In fact, those He chose were despised, considered to be morons, ill-bred, and insignificant by most people (1 Corinthians 1:26-28). God chose the nobodies to guide the somebodies to His body. It is time we understood that the Scripture says we are to associate with the lowly and to quit thinking we are so "above" others (Romans 12:16).

Even Jesus was not particularly handsome or pleasant to look upon. The prophets foretold that Jesus would have no stately form or handsome appearance that would cause people to be attracted to Him by His magnetic looks (Isaiah 53:2). Jesus, from the human standards, was a nobody. One of the criticisms hurled at Him was that He was "just a carpenter's son." They were meaning that He did not have the proper background (Matthew 13:54-56). They took offense at Him as one from the wrong side of the tracks (13:57). How blinded we become if we look at the outward appearance only!

John the Baptist

There is a world of difference between the way we do things and the way God does things. Christ did not come from the castle, but from the cradle in the barn. His messenger, John, did not come dressed in cashmere, but in camel's hair. Wouldn't we be surprised to discover that God continues to use the lowly? How much have we missed by brushing aside, through negligence, the ill-bred, the insignificant odd people in our communities? How many potential John the Baptists have we squelched?

It is not the countenance and clothes but the character and commitment that make the difference. Jesus taught us that we must not make food and clothing our priorities. We must value character much more (Matthew 6:25-33). In our materialistic society, it is easy to forget what our priorities must be. It is hard not to judge others the same way the world judges them, that is, by outward appearance. We must instead get to know the inside capacities of our brothers and sisters, their attitudes, character, and commitment.

John's Greatness

How could God use an oddity like John the Baptist so significantly? I feel that there are three interrelated factors:

(1) God gave John a *challenge*.

(2) God gave John his *commitment*.

(3) The people gave John a *chance*.

God worded His challenge about John even before John was born: "He will be great" in the sight of the Lord. Why? Because he will be moral (no drinking), spiritual (filled with the Holy Spirit), and motivating (turning many to the Lord). John also would be a preparer for another (Luke 1:14-17).

As John matured he commited himself to being great in the sight of the Lord, and no more. He wanted to be great in the sight of God only. He resisted any pressure to be great in the sight of men.

John lived a life of unquestionable morality. He

maintained a strict diet without either bread or wine (Luke 7:33). Evidently he fasted often, prayed regularly, and he taught his disciples to do the same (Luke 5:33; 11:1). A few said he had a demon (7:33), but more said he was the Messiah and a prophet (Matthew 16:14; John 1:20, 25).

The people gave John a chance. They came to hear this man who obviously was filled with dedication to God. John took advantage of this opportunity to elevate God and His will, not his own. He pointed many from himself to Jesus. John's philosophy was "turn the spotlight on Jesus, not on me. I'm just a *voice.* Jesus is the *power.*" John had the mark of true greatness.

John's Message

The crowds thronged to hear John. Why? Not because he was doing spectacular things. He did not perform one sign (John 10:41). He drew the crowds simply through his preaching. How refreshing! The people came to hear great preaching. They did not need gimmicks.

Yet John never watered down his message, or tickled the ears of his hearers. He baptized where there was *much* water (John 3:23). He wasn't known as John the Baptizer for no reason. While many are embarrassed with immersion today, John demanded it. His preaching was not emotional, geared to provoke tears, nor to psychologically force people to "make decisions" that could be numbered. No, John called for *real* repentance: "Repent, for the kingdom of heaven is at hand" (Matthew 3:2). He talked about repentance *before* he talked about Heaven or baptism.

When some came to be baptized just to insure themselves a safe place in eternity, John said, "No deal! You are not getting a baptismal certificate from me unless you repent first." When some tried to fool John by saying they would repent while never intending to, he scathingly demanded, "Show me first the

27

fruits that demonstrate you have repented" (Matthew 3:7, 8).*

Your life must square with your confession. Without repentance, you will be cut down, just like a tree that does not bear fruit. It does not matter how "wet" you are or what station in life you maintain. This was John's declaration and what he expected as results (Matthew 3:10).

When some people asked what they would have to do to prove their repentance (Luke 3:10), John did not dodge the question, beat around the bush, or ask, "What do you think?" He said, "Change your lives!" Those who are stingy, become generous. Those who cheat for gain, quit it. Those who complain about their pay, stop whining and become content. Those who are in authority and who like to show brutality, become gentle (Luke 3:10-14).

What would happen in our churches today if we demanded repentance before baptism? They would grow. What do we do to the church when we fire the preacher for demanding repentance and taking a stand against immorality? We weaken it.

At the start of this decade, seventy-five percent of the people who were polled concerning whether they thought the church was necessary said no. The reason they gave for their answer was that immorality is on the increase. The point is that the church becomes repulsive to people when we tone down demands for moral responsibilities.

John's Commitment

What a paradox we see in John. On the one hand, he had personal morality. He lived by himself in the desert and did not attend any social parties. On the other hand, he did not have the common hermit's outlook on society. He was concerned about social responsibility. He spoke about giving to the poor, being honest, and not mistreating people. The nobody challenged the somebodies, and they knew he was right. They started changing, and society became prepared for the unveiling of the Messiah.

John would not live to see the Messiah's conquering of the last enemy, because his call for repentance went right to the top of society: the government. It cost him his life. He did not sidetrack or cover up the "Watergates" of his time with the excuse that politics and religion don't mix. John exposed *all* the wicked things the governor was doing. Living in sexual immorality was just one item on the list (Luke 3:19, 20).

John never backed down on his stand for morality. He would not invite Herod to speak at his evangelistic meetings to increase the crowds and get proper press coverage. Herod would have to change, just as everyone else. There was no privileged class.

John was very popular, but he was not an opportunist. He refused to bend his message, and he would not change his clothing in order to better fit in with society. Jesus himself made these points clear: "What was it that drew you to the wilderness? Reeds blown by the wind? What was it you wanted to see? A man dressed in fine clothing? Men who wear fine clothes are found in palaces. But what did you *really* go out there to see, a prophet? Yes, a prophet—" (Matthew 11:7-9).*

Isn't it time people flocked to the services to hear the Word of God preached fearlessly again? It is so easy to start changing our priorities when acceptance and popularity come our way. The more we are recognized the more sensitive we can become to how we look and sound. Are we dressing in the latest style? Will we create instant rapport? It is all right to be concerned about these things as long as we do not shift our priorities.

Even as John's popularity grew, he refused to be pressed into any mold other than what he was dedicated to be—a voice in the wilderness. It would have been a temptation to want to sit on a pedestal when the people were ready to put him there. But John kept refusing honors. He was not seeking honorary degrees. He was selected to be a voice, and this was all he wanted (John 1:20-23).

John was committed to point to Jesus: "I am not worthy to untie Jesus' sandals" (John 1:27)*; "Behold, the Lamb of God who takes away the sin of the world!" (1:29); "After me comes a man who has a higher rank than I" (v. 30); "This is the Son of God" (v. 34); "He must increase, but I must decrease" (3:30); "He who believes in the Son has eternal life; but he who does not obey the Son shall not see life, but the wrath of God abides on him" (v. 36).

What a messenger for God! He would not let the elevated opinions surrounding him elevate his own opinion of himself. He impressed people, but not once did he seek that as his goal. His goal was to be great in the sight of God and to do His will. He did not need credit from his fellowmen.

John's commitment and humble attitude resulted in a commendation from Jesus, "Truly, I say to you, among those born of women there has not arisen anyone greater than John the Baptist" (Matthew 11:11). What a compliment from the Lord himself!

But wait a minute! He added, "Yet he who is least in the kingdom of heaven is greater than he" (Matthew 11:11). Jesus began talking about you and me. We can be greater than John the Baptist!

Before we let that go to our heads, however, let's match God's challenge that we are greater by exhibiting the commitment to be great in the sight of God. Let us give each other a chance to develop potentialities for God, regardless of background, dress, or where we live.

Let us look beyond a man's diet to his dedication, beyond his clothes to his character, beyond his face to his heart. Let us give each other a chance to be great in the sight of God. Let us each have a humble attitude: "He must increase, and I must decrease."

30

The Thunderclouds

Why in the world did Jesus pick *them* to be His followers? One would have been more than enough, but *two*?

James and John were brothers and seemed to be "out of the same mold." They grew up together and no doubt played together. They were together so much that they seemed to think and act just alike. By the time they were adults, apparently they agreed on every issue. They worked together on the same job (fishing) and at the same place (their father's business).

When Jesus confronted the brothers with His call and challenge, they left their father's business *together*. I doubt that either one of them made the decision independently of the other. I can just see them looking at each other, nodding, simultaneously laying down their nets, and walking off with Jesus, side by side.

From that time on, until after the resurrection of Jesus, we seldom see one of them without the other. It is usually James *and* John.

Thunderous Reactions

James and John grew up in a family that had hired servants (Mark 1:20). Their mother, Salome, seemed to be one of the women who could leave the household duties to hired servants, travel with Jesus, and support His ministry financially (Luke 8:1-3; Matthew 27:55; Mark 15:40), 41).

Certainly there is nothing wrong about growing

James and John

up in a rich family, but these two boys were spoiled. They remained spoiled as men traveling with Jesus. Evidently they had been used to teaming up to get their way around home. They probably had their mother wrapped around their fingers, and used her to get their way with their father.

When they did not get their way, they threw temper tantrums. Jesus realized that right away and nicknamed them "sons of thunder" (Mark 3:17). When they did not get their way, they became like human tornadoes unleashed and aimed right at the obstacles standing in their way.

We see a classic example of their stormy reactions in Luke 9:51-56. Jesus and the apostles were traveling from Galilee to Jerusalem. Instead of bypassing Samaria, as many Jews did, they went right through it. Samaria was a biracial area, and racial tensions were hot. The Jews hated the Samaritans, and the Samaritans hated the Jews. Traveling through Samaria was as uncomfortable for some Jews as driving through a ghetto area is for some middle-class whites today; but Jesus was not uncomfortable walking through that area.

The day had been long, the sun was beginning to set, and Jerusalem was still a long way off. They could not possibly reach it that day. Jesus sent James and John ahead into a certain village to reserve rooms in the Samaritan version of the Holiday Inn.

I can practically hear them talking as they approach the Inn: "Hey, this is a nice place. Am I ready for a rest!"

"Yea, and look at the swimming pool. I can't wait to take a dip."

"We're in luck. There are only five donkeys parked outside. Must be plenty of available rooms."

But then the boom was lowered! When they asked for the rooms, the innkeeper noted their race and their destination, Jerusalem (9:53), and told them there was no vacancy.

33

The sons of thunder must have responded, "What? What do you mean, no room? You've got to be kidding! There are only five donkeys parked outside, and there is no one in the pool. Your inn is not full!"

"But we have an ordinance: no one of your kind can stay in this village overnight."

The tornadoes were beginning to form and move in on the target. James and John ran back to Jesus in anger and bitterness, "Do You want us to command fire to come down from heaven and consume them?" (9:54). They were ready to do it, and they wanted to do it. They wanted to wipe out the whole village—men, women, children, dogs, cats—the whole lot.

How disappointed they must have been when Jesus put out their fire with a rebuke (9:55). They had traveled with Jesus all this time and yet had not allowed His kind of reaction to opposition to become theirs. In fact, some later manuscripts record Jesus as saying to them, "You do not know what kind of spirit you are of." Instead of living by the sword of the Spirit, they were living by the spirit of the sword.

Jesus' reaction to the innkeeper's refusal was so beautiful. We simply read, "And they went on to another village" (9:56). James and John had a long way to go before that type of protection became theirs. They were like babies who needed to grow up.

What about us? Are our reactions showing, or are Jesus' reactions showing through us? How do we handle rejection or mistreatment? Are we like the sons of thunder when the red light changes and the guy behind us lays on the horn? How do you handle it when the wife brings home the car after shopping, and then it runs out of gas when you have gone a couple of miles down the road?

James and John could not stand competition. They had been used to holding all the marbles in their bags at home. When they noticed that some others were casting out demons who did not have member-

34

ship in their group, they could think of just one thing—stop them (Mark 9:38)! Again Jesus admonishes the brothers to replace the spirit of the sword with the sword of the Spirit (9:39-41).

How do we handle competition between groups? I think one of the greatest factors hindering world evangelism is our group competition and lack of recognition of one another as brothers and sisters in Christ. We see friction on every hand. Two congregations of the same faith in the same town seldom, if ever, work toward helping the other's program succeed.

What would happen if people from one congregation joined in the calling program of another's evangelistic endeavor? Is a handful of people attending one night of a revival a clear indication to the community that we are "one"?

I know of situations where preachers will never announce activities that a sister congregation is having. A speaker can come into an area and speak to only one church. Before he leaves, the preacher from another congregation a mile down the road asks the same speaker to return to speak at his church at a later time on the same subject. Sometimes we simply ignore the doings of the other church, but often we go a step farther and undermine their programs.

Our thunderclouds really begin to form if the other congregation is of a different "faith." Do we really believe that there is no one in that congregation who could be our brother or sister? Is it possible that we don't have to agree on every minor point to be a part of God's family? Is it possible that we spend a lot of energy trying to evangelize people who are already in the family? There is a little bit of James and John in all of us.

The Stars

Having temper tantrums was not the only problem that James and John had. They also wanted to be

35

the "stars." They had been accustomed to being in the spotlight at home, and now they wanted to be the favorite ones in Jesus' group. They had tried to squirm their way into the two top positions, but hadn't succeeded. So they used a tactic that probably had worked many times at home. They got their mother to speak to Jesus for them. After all, she ought to have a lot of influence, especially if she was the sister of Mary, Jesus' mother, as many scholars agree (John 19:25; Matthew 27:56).

Jesus' explanation about greatness was revealing (20:25-28). He made it clear that greatness does not come by planning for it and grabbing it at the expense of others. That remark in itself probably gives us a clue as to how James and John had been acting. The other apostles were very upset (20:24), so Jesus assured them that such an approach does not get the desired results from God.

How can we become great, then? By unselfishly being a slave to others, to spend time and energy elevating others (20:26, 27). James and John would have to break out of their mold to become great. That is just what Jesus wanted to see happen. He wanted them to change their violent attitudes to those of gentleness and caring. He knew that the best way for them to change was to see in Him the right kind of model for their lives (20:28).

Have you ever wondered why Peter, James, and John were selected to spend private times with Jesus (Mark 5:37; 9:2; 14:33)? Certainly not because Jesus "played favorites." I rather suspect it was because these three needed to be exposed to more of Jesus' example and gentle character than some of the other apostles.

Jesus knew in what areas they needed to mature. He did not like their attitudes, but He certainly loved those men. In fact, John is probably the one referred to as the disciple whom Jesus loved (John 13:23).

That should give us a lot of hope. There is much

in our lives that Jesus does not like, but He loves us. We don't have to put on a mask or act a part to get His approval. He loves us the way we are. He does not reserve His love or His involvement in our lives until we reach a level of maturity that would not embarrass Him. He is not intimidated by our immaturity. He does not want to throw the spiritual babies out with the baptismal water.

Jesus was not even threatened by the thought that these two hotheads would give the group a bad reputation. He could see what they would become. He knew He had to spend time with them to bridge the gap between them and Him. To isolate them would be to leave them too much to each other. They would imitate each other instead of Jesus.

That is an example for us. We should not stay away from those who are not as mature as we are. We should associate with them and become their models of maturity. They need that exposure. There is no danger of overexposure to Christlikeness, but there is definite danger of underexposure.

Growing Toward Christ

To observe the lives of James and John is like watching a movie about spiritual growth. The two who wanted to become the stars listened to Jesus talk about greatness and service. Soon John took on the menial task of getting things ready for the Passover feast, and he didn't have to have James along (Luke 22:8). That was a rather lowly task for the guy who had just asked to be one of the top dogs of the kingdom.

The brothers were growing. They were learning to think as individuals. Jesus even left the care of His mother to John (John 19:26, 27). John didn't feel threatened that Peter was given the keys to the kingdom and was told to feed the sheep (Matthew 16:18, 19; John 21:15-17). In fact, he worked very closely with Peter after the resurrection of Jesus. In Acts we read of Peter and John, not James and John (3:3).

The brothers grew so they could work with others in the kingdom without each other. They no longer needed to team up or seek to get their way. They had changed!

James, who wanted to destroy opposition, was the first of the apostles to be killed, and he did not resist. The sword of the Spirit had won (Acts 12:1, 2)!

John, who once had such a hot temper wrote more about love than did any of the other apostles. He recorded Jesus' magnificent commission: "A new commandment I give to you, that you love one another, even as I have loved you . . . By this all men will know that you are My disciples, if you have love for one another" (John 13:34, 35).

Only John recorded Jesus' saying, "Abide in My love" (John 15:9). Only John recorded Jesus' prayer that God's children be as united as Jesus is with the Father (John 17). He was no longer the man who could not stand it when others who were not in his group were doing things for God.

It was only John who wrote, "If someone says, 'I love God,' and hates his brother, he is a liar; for the one who does not love his brother whom he has seen, cannot love God whom he has not seen" (1 John 4:20). Quite a different attitude from wanting to call down fire from Heaven to consume a village!

John, who had wanted to fight back when wronged, told Christians not to fight back, but to trust God to whom all vengeance belongs. He wrote of love and victory, even though he was exiled to the Isle of Patmos.

History records that John died at an old age in Ephesus. His body weakened to the point that he had to be carried on a pallet to the assembly of Christians. Every time the assembly met, John was asked if he had a word for the Christians. Each time he would have the same words, "Brothers, love one another."

John was no longer a son of thunder. He had grown into a mature son of God. He became a living example of Jesus' beatitude, "Blessed are the peacemakers, for they shall be called sons of God" (Matthew 5:9).

Such maturity did not happen overnight. James and John started out as spoiled babies, but became selfless brothers to everyone. They no longer looked out for just each other but also for all others. They began to think and act as Jesus did.

They grew because Jesus did not give up on them. He spent time with them. He showed them the perfect model of maturity. He did not step down to their level of maturity to keep rapport with them. He took them aside for special occasions, so they could notice His actions and reactions at close range. He gave them responsibility, and He disciplined them when they were wrong. Jesus saw what the brothers could become and was determined to help them become that.

But James and John had to become open to change. They were spoiled, but they were teachable. Just a small opening for Jesus' influence to shine in— that was all He needed.

Each of us needs to ask the questions: Where is the opening in my life? Am I allowing enough room for Jesus to influence me? Am I trapped in the prison house of "This is the way I've always been, and this is the way I'm going to remain. I can't change and I won't change"?

Jesus is standing at the door of your hearts knocking. If anyone hears His voice and opens the door, He will come in and dine with him (Revelation 3:20). There is growing power in the fellowship with Jesus.

Be willing to change, so you can reach the target of maturity!

Andrew

The Star
and the Stagehand

As different as night and day, as opposite as sunrise and sunset, as diverse as the colors of the rainbow, were the two brothers, Andrew and Peter. Peter was always at the head of the line bragging about himself. Andrew was always back in the crowd, getting acquainted with the people.

Peter would tell Jesus what he knew. Andrew would tell others whom he knew—Jesus. Peter was full of prejudice, while Andrew felt no guile toward any man. He brought Gentiles to Jesus (John 12:20-22), but it took ten more years for Peter to have that open attitude (Acts 10). They also left their nets together to follow Jesus, but there was no way these two brothers could act as a team or think or act alike, until they matured in Jesus.

Andrew

Every time we read of Andrew, he seems to be running his own social service agency. He is always helping compatible people associate and work together. To do this, he had to have a well-rounded, agreeable personality. He had to be the type of person people trusted and felt comfortable with. Even Peter, who was so different from him, trusted Andrew's judgment. When Andrew exclaimed, "We have found the Messiah!" (John 1:40, 41) Peter followed him to Jesus.

41

Who would notice a lone little boy in a crowd of ten thousand or more (five thousand plus women and children)? Who would pay attention to a kid sitting by himself at an event as busy as the state fair? Andrew would, that's who. He always mingled with the crowd. He did not sit on the platform with the speaker. As the day wore on, Andrew had met many of the people and knew much about them. He listened; he paid attention; he cared. He was not like many of us who pretend we are listening when in reality we are planning what we are going to say next.

When the question was asked, "Where will we get food to feed these people?" Andrew had a partial answer: "I've met a lad who has a little food" (John 6:5-9).* Andrew got the boy and Jesus together. At another time, some Greeks wanted to talk with Jesus. Andrew and his social consciousness went to work. Philip brought them to him, he gained their confidence, and introduced them to Jesus (12:20-22).

Andrew cared about people, not praise. He was willing to take a back seat, even to Peter, his own brother. Andrew is mentioned only twelve times in the New Testament, and four of those times are in the list with the other apostles. Peter is mentioned 160 times, but many of those times dealt with Peter's problems. He had a lot more growing up to do than did Andrew.

Most of the time, Andrew is referred to as Peter's brother. How would you like to be introduced always as the brother or sister of someone? We can learn from Andrew. He didn't mind such a designation at all. He lived to elevate others. He worked behind the scenes and introduced people to Jesus, people who later got more attention and publicity than he.

There are a lot of "Andrews" in our churches today—those people who stay in the wings, making it possible for others to remain on the stage in the spotlight. These people are needed and very valuable. Remember, if Andrew had not introduced Peter to Jesus, there would have been no great and fiery preacher. We all cannot be the same, or do the same for Jesus, but we all can use our different personalities and abilities to serve the same Lord.

Peter

It is not hard to understand how God could use a man like Andrew, but what about Peter? If God could use Peter, then there is hope for you and me.

Peter was an arrogant, bragging, boisterous, impulsive know-it-all who looked out for himself. He had a heap of growing up to do when he met Jesus. He needed special attention and much exposure to Jesus, as did James and John.

Jesus nicknamed Peter "Rock" when He first met him (John 1:42). A rock signifies someone hard and determined, which certainly described Peter. When Peter made up his mind, it was made up!

This quality can be good or bad. It can be good if one's mind is made up on what is right and true. Then the winds of time and change will not alter it. It would be bad if one's mind is made up on what is false, for then he is stubborn and blind to the truth. Christianity began with the challenge to change: "Repent." If a person is unchangeable, he can neither be born again nor grow into the likeness of Jesus.

Anyone who is stubborn and stuck on himself can learn many lessons from Peter. Regardless of how hard a man's shell may appear, there usually is a soft spot somewhere. Peter liked to appear as hard and determined as a rock, but he had a soft spot. There were times when he acted more like a marshmallow. He was concrete, but the cement had not completely settled. An impression could still be made on him, and Jesus began to impress His footprints into the soft spots of the cement of Peter's heart.

Peter did change, and what a beautiful process it was! If it could happen to Peter, it can happen to any man or woman in your community, a nonchurchgoer or a long-standing member of the church board.

The Growth Process

Peter was a know-it-all who had to have the last word. He thought he knew more than the teacher. "I dare you to teach me anything" seemed to be his attitude. He seemed to be on a mental coffee break many of the times Jesus was teaching.

All through His ministry, Jesus taught that He himself would be rejected by the religious leaders and be killed, but He would rise again. The apostles listened, but Peter raised his hand and blurted out, "Teacher, You are wrong about that. Nothing like that is going to happen to You. You should have checked with me before making such a statement" (Mark 8:31, 32).* Jesus had to put Peter in his place by saying, in essence, "Peter, will you sit down and be quiet? Don't forget who the Teacher is and who the student is! Get your head on straight!" (Mark 8:33).*

Another time, Peter cricitized Jesus' question. Jesus and the apostles were walking in the midst of a heavy crowd when a diseased woman touched Jesus' garment for healing (Luke 8:43, 44). Jesus knew that someone had touched Him, someone who had a special need. He asked, "Who is the one who touched Me?" (v. 45).

"Now, what kind of question is that?" thought Peter, looking at the throngs of people crowding around and touching Jesus. Peter, with his calculated logic, answered, "Well, in this crowd, who *hasn't* touched You? Let's keep going!" (v. 45).* Peter needed to learn that the student was not above his teacher and that the student was to strive to become like the teacher (Luke 6:40).

Peter looked out for himself, first and foremost. One time he asked Jesus if forgiving a person seven times was enough. Peter did not want to do any more forgiving than he had to. But Jesus knocked the breath out of him when He answered, "You should forgive seventy times seven" (Matthew 18:22).* Who is going to keep track of that many times? That

44

Simon Peter

was Jesus' whole point. "Throw away your record book, Peter."

Peter continued to try to teach the Teacher how to handle situations. Jesus taught that there was to be no resistance to His arrest, but Peter thought Jesus was wrong about that. He pulled out a sword and started swinging when the soldiers came to get Jesus. Jesus was willing to give His blood, but Peter wanted to spill the blood of others (John 18:10). After Jesus' arrest, Peter looked out for his own interests and became a marshmallow instead of a rock. He followed Jesus from a distance (Mark 14:54). He did not want others to think he was connected with the arrested Man.

In the yard outside the courtroom, an insignificant maiden said, "This man was with Him too" (Luke 22:56). The brave, strong, and stalwart Peter said, "Woman, I do not know Him" (v. 57).

Somewhat later another said, "You are one of them, too," and with the same bravado Peter declared, "Man, I am not."

An hour later, Peter had another chance to show what he was made of, and he turned out to be a marshmallow: "Man, I do not know what you are talking about" (v. 60). And this was after spending three years with the Son of God! Was there no hope for Peter?

Even after the resurrection, Peter was still looking out for himself. Jesus had just given him the tough assignment, "Feed my sheep." Peter looked back at another disciple and wanted to know what he was going to do (John 21:21). Jesus again put Peter in his place. "What is that to you?" (21:22). Peter needed to hear that, in order to get on with what he could offer to God.

How many of us need to hear that same thing? So what if another person is doing less than you? What is that to you? Or what if another is doing more than you and getting so much recognition for it? What is that to you? You have a task to do. Don't stumble over the other person!

All the while and all through these things, Peter was growing. On one occasion, he admitted that he was a sinful man (Luke 5:8). That was the first step, breaking down selfish pride.

At another time, he came to realize he couldn't succeed in everything just by his own will power. Jesus was walking on the water and said, "It is I." Peter challenged Him, "If it is You, command me to come to You on the water" (Matthew 14:27, 28). Jesus beckoned him, so Peter began walking on the water, but he let the wind scare him, and he began to sink. Peter learned that he could succeed with Jesus, but would sink without Him.

On another occasion, Peter demonstrated another important attitude. He and others had been fishing all night but had caught nothing. Jesus told them to go out into the deep water and let down their nets for a catch (Luke 5:4). His instructions were against any of the common-sense tactics of an experienced fisherman. After all, they had been fishing all night. Should they listen to a carpenter? But Peter said, "At Your bidding I will let down the nets."

Peter acted even against his own common sense because Jesus told him to do so. When there is a command of God staring us in the face, we should obey, even if it is against logic or the way we were brought up. Only with this kind of faith can we continue to grow.

Peter grew by leaps and bounds. Only a few weeks after he had denied knowing Jesus to an insignificant maiden, he declared before the significant masters of the land that he would not shut up talking about Jesus (Acts 4:19, 20). Christianity was facing annihilation, for Peter and John were warned not to speak at all anymore to any man in the name of Jesus (4:17, 18). Now that meant *zero* talk about Jesus, even in their own group.

After this warning, Peter and John went to a prayer meeting and prayed for boldness to keep on speaking about Jesus (4:31). They continued to do what the rulers of the land told them not to do. Peter and John were put in prison because of it (5:17, 18), and God released them (5:19). They were told to quit speaking, but God told them to stand and speak to the people in the temple and tell them the whole message of the new life (5:20).

Peter and John were arrested again and beaten severely. They were again ordered to speak no more in the name of Jesus (5:40). They continued to preach Jesus Christ every day in public and in private (5:42). And Peter led the way!

When things got tough, Peter did not think about watering down the truth or abandoning it. What did he speak about? Not himself, but Jesus! He no longer just thought of himself! He was pointing others to Jesus! Still, he was not fully mature. Peter had been a segregationist all of his life. He would have voted for a segregated church. He would not have even set foot inside a Gentile's home. He had seen how Jesus crossed racial barriers, and he had heard the Great Commission to go into all the world and speak to every person (Matthew 28:19, 20; Luke 24:47). But Peter's prejudice blinded him from comprehending that "all the world" and "every creature" actually meant that "other race."

It is so difficult to see through prejudice when you are taught it in the home, the school, and the church (Acts 13:27). Peter could not put it aside, even after three years with Jesus. Years after he had been preaching boldly and was clearly ready to die for his faith, he continued his segregationist feelings and practices. He could even turn to the Scriptures to support his attitude.

No doubt you all know of someone who is mature in the faith, but who is still a staunch segregationist. Not every part of a person's character matures at the same rate. In this area of his life, Peter had not grown one inch.

It took a special vision from God before Peter finally broke with his past. The vision included all sorts of animals. God told him to kill and eat them (Acts 10:10-13). When Peter saw the food as ethnically related, he thought about the people connected with that food. Just as we think about a certain people when we hear "chop suey" or "pizza," he thought of the Gentiles when he saw pork. To eat that food would mean Peter could associate with those people, even eat with them! Peter again challenged the teaching of his Master. "By no means, Lord" (v. 14). The Lord was so patient. He kept prodding Peter so he would understand. Peter finally realized that God was telling him that he should associate with Gentiles (10:28, 34, 35.)

After this, Peter proceeded to do so. Not only did he evangelize them, but when they asked him to "stay on" for a few days, he consented. This meant that he stayed in their home, slept between their sheets, and ate their food (vv. 34-48). He made it clear that God is no segregationist.

Peter was criticized for this (11:1-3), but he did not back down (11:4-17). Of course, it is not easy to put aside prejudice, and it is not done overnight. Peter went through a period when he moved back and forth on the racial issue. He ate with Gentiles as long as there weren't any Jews around to know about it. When Jews appeared, he turned away from the Gentiles. Integration is toughest when the segregationists are looking. Before, Peter would have been a part of the Klu Klux Klan against Gentiles; so when the Klan members came snooping around, he got nervous (Galatians 2:11-13).

But Peter was mature in many ways. Evidently he took Paul's rebuke in a good spirit (vv. 13-21), for later when Jewish Christians met to discuss the racial issue, Peter stood before them and advocated strongly accepting and fellowshiping with the Gentile Christians (Acts 15:7-11).

I imagine that many church members are as determined about the racial issue as Peter was. It is extremely difficult to overcome prejudice, but God certainly considers this an area of needed growth. He wants His children on earth to live with each other the way we will live together in Heaven.

Who are we to mock God's creation? Who are we to suggest that some people He created are inferior and others are superior? God will not send us a vision as He did to Peter. Instead He shares with us the written revelation of that vision and expects us to learn from it.

God was patient with Peter's prejudices, and Peter was willing to change when he saw clearly that his stance was not God's. We may be every bit as prejudiced as Peter was, but are we as open to change as he was? It was not easy for Peter to sit down and eat with a person of another race. He was uncomfortable and his stomach was queasy. But he was willing to grow in *every* aspect toward Jesus, God's target for him.

The Final Step

The Peter we see in 1 and 2 Peter is not the same Peter that we read about in the Gospels. The gap between his character and that of Jesus had narrowed. Peter, who was so self-willed in the Gospels, warned his readers to watch out for the self-willed (2 Peter 2:10). He who thought he knew more than the Teacher, wrote that his readers should remember "the words spoken beforehand by the holy prophets and the commandment of the Lord and Savior" (3:2). Peter became the fulfilled student, teaching only what Jesus taught.

The Peter who had wanted to cut off the ear of his opponent wrote that Christians should bear up "under sorrows when suffering unjustly" (1 Peter 2:19). He said his readers should follow Jesus' example of non-retaliation (1 Peter 2:21-23). Peter, who had wanted to be the boss, wrote to the elders not to lord it over the flock (1 Peter 5:3). Peter, who had wanted people to think he had all the answers, wrote his last words urging people to "grow in the grace and knowledge of our Lord and Savior Jesus Christ" (2 Peter 3:18).

From pride to humility, from thinking of self to thinking of Christ and others—how Peter did grow!

Tradition tells us that Peter died by being crucified upside down. It is recorded that he requested it to be done in that manner because he was not worthy to die in the same fashion as his Lord. That is coming a long way from his babyhood when he tried to tell Jesus what was what. Peter was a diamond in the rough who was brushed and polished by the Master's hand. Jesus could see his potentialities sparkle beneath all the mud.

Jesus can see the diamond in you also. He can brush off the mud and polish you. It takes a lot of time, but are you willing? Can you take the steps that Peter took to grow?

(1) I admit that I am a sinful person.

(2) I will sink without Jesus' help.

(3) What God commands, I will do.

Heed the advice of Peter:

"Applying all diligence, in your faith supply moral excellence, and in your moral excellence, knowledge: and in your knowledge, self-control, and in your self-control, perseverance, and in your perseverance, godliness; and in your godliness, brotherly kindness, and in your brotherly kindness, Christian love. For if these qualities are yours and are increasing, they render you neither useless nor unfruitful in the true knowledge of our Lord Jesus Christ" (2 Peter 1:5-8).

Barnabas

The People-Booster

"Up with people" was the motto of Barnabas. He was a supporter and encourager of people. He had the knack for seeing good in people when no one else could. When other people purposely shied away from someone, Barnabas would just as purposely move in alongside of him. He sought to bring out the best in people, even if it meant he would receive criticism, or be left out of the "in" group.

Barnabas spotted potential rockets for God and lit their fuses. He did not care for one second when they soared far beyond him. His ministry was fulfilled by spotting others with potential and putting them on a launching pad for God. He gave people a chance when others would not.

This was so much a part of Barnabas' life-style that the first time he is mentioned in Scripture he is referred to as Joseph, but called "Barnabas," which means "Son of Encouragement" (Acts 4:36; NASB).

It is easy for us to become sons of discouragement rather than encouragement. All we have to do is think negatively. This will blind us to the good that there is in people.

A story is told of two farmers who lived side by side. One always looked at the dark side of things, the other at the bright side. One farmer would say, "Isn't it a beautiful day?" The other would say, "Yes, but if the sun keeps shining like that, it will burn up the crops."

One would say, "Isn't this a blessed rain we're having?" The other would say, "Yes, but if this keeps up, we'll have a flood."

53

I am afraid many of us get caught in that same trap. Just bring up a name in a conversation, and someone will invariably say, "Yes, but—" Preachers are masters at this. It is hard to let someone get credit without putting in a bit of criticism.

How do you score? Notice how many times in the next week you say or get ready to say something negative about someone. You can stop it if you notice you are doing it.

Encourager Of The Poor

It did not matter to Barnabas what kind of people they were, he encouraged and supported them. The first time we read about him in Scripture, he was helping the poverty-stricken Christians in his area (Acts 4:34-37).

Many Jews in Jerusalem had become Christians, and this created a serious economic problem. Many lost their jobs because their employers were Jews, and they were not sympathetic with Christianity, to put it mildly. Some of these were businessmen who lost their customers when they changed religions. Widows who were converted were taken off the Jewish welfare program lists.

Needless to say, these Christians were discouraged, but Barnabas was there to encourage. He did not just say, "Cheer up! Things could be worse." He went into action. He sold some of his real estate and gave it all to help his Christian brothers.

Encourager Of A Newcomer

When Paul was converted, he began preaching, which upset the Jews, and he had to escape from Damascus by night to save his life (Acts 9:1-25). Where could he go? Of course, he went to Jerusalem to associate with the disciples and apostles; but no one would have anything to do with him (9:26). They did not trust him because he had been a persecutor of the Christians. They did not believe that he could be a

54

true disciple. Paul needed a friend to break down the barriers of unfamiliarity, doubt, and mistrust.

Barnabas was that friend. He moved in alongside of Paul and broke down the feelings of fear and apprehension (9:27). He helped the group welcome this newcomer. Then Paul was able to stay with the Christians, move freely among them, and preach boldly for Christ.

Look around your congregation. Is there a newcomer who as yet does not feel welcome? Is there someone who seems isolated and lonely? Perhaps you can be a "Barnabas" to that person. Get acquainted, stay with him, help move him into the inner circles of activity. It takes time and patience, but what a ministry!

Encourager Of A Church

When the first racially integrated congregation began (Acts 11:19-21), Barnabas was the natural choice to send to that congregation (11:22, 23). Others would have put a damper on the project by saying, "It never has been done that way before." Others would have been negative and closed to new ideas.

How did Barnabas handle the situation? First, he sized things up before he made a judgment. He knew that this was a unique congregation and it would have unique problems. He did not make up his mind what he was going to do even before he got there. He was not quick to condemn or criticize. He was sensitive to God's perspectives about people and situations. Thus, he was able to see the grace of God working in Antioch (11:23).

Then he began to encourage them all. The result? People in great numbers were added to that congregation (11:24). In fact, the church grew so rapidly that Barnabas sent for someone to work full time. He sent for a man who, as far as we know, had no experience working in a located church. He had preached a few places, but had not stayed long. He had no proven, workable program for building a congregation. He had never worked in a *new* church, let alone one that was racially integrated. In fact, he had "dropped out of sight." Barnabas had a hard time finding him (11:25; the word "look" in the Greek indicates looking with some difficulty).

The congregation would have asked, "Who are you looking for, Barnabas? Paul? Paul who?" Barnabas wanted to put Paul back into circulation and help the church at the same time. He did the right thing, for both the church and Paul prospered.

Just look at the results: the church at Antioch is probably the one church in the New Testament that deserves being imitated. It did not close its doors to any race. It is not that they didn't have problems, either. They must have had a heap of problems when Jews and Gentiles worshiped together. The first pitch-in dinner with pork on the table would create enough problems to split any congregation!

This congregation balanced local evangelism (vv. 21, 24) with edification (v. 26), benevolence (vv. 29, 30), and worldwide evangelism (13:1-3). They had the cream of the crop on their ministerial staff. Did they beg these people to stay, or raise their salaries so they would not be tempted to leave? No, instead they thought about how their church had grown in knowledge and numbers, and they wanted others to be exposed to these men and their message.

Does your congregation have a preacher who needs to be building up other Christians across the nation, either through speaking or writing? What are you doing about it? Do you limit him to a week's meeting and only two Sundays a year to be away? How are you allowing him to contribute to the worldwide family of God?

If you have someone on your staff who needs to multiply his or her ministry by traveling or writing, encourage that person. Be unselfish with your personnel. I am thinking specifically of a church in Fullerton,

California, who shares the preacher, Ben Merold, with the nation; and how that church is growing!

Why not be a "Barnabas" to your neighboring Bible college? Encourage the administration to allow some of their teachers to write. We desperately need Christian writers, but Bible college professors have three times the teaching load of university professors, and have little time to write. How about underwriting the wages of one or two professors while they spend time in writing and teaching only part-time? In that way you would be supporting Christian journalism.

Encourager Of A Fellow Worker

Barnabas continued his encouragement when he traveled with Paul. We read about "Barnabas and Paul" in that order. At one location, Barnbas was given top billing by being compared to Zeus ("chief god"), while Paul was compared to Hermes ("chief speaker for Zeus"; Acts 14:12). It wasn't long before the Scriptures referred to them as "Paul and Barnabas" in that order (15:2). Barnabas was then second on the bill, but he did not mind.

It takes a mature person to encourage a fellow worker and then stand aside as that person surpasses him in popularity. Barnabas would rather boost up someone else than receive any honors. He was not competitive or jealous. Paul could have received many honorary doctorates, and Barnabas would have rejoiced with him every time. I can just see Barnabas passing out Paul's writings everywhere he went!

Encourager Of A Quitter

Although Barnabas helped Paul, he did not always agree with Paul. He had discovered someone else with potential. He was not going to allow the influence of anyone, not even Paul, to prevent him from giving the boost Mark needed. Barnabas stood up for Paul in front of the apostles, then he had to stand up against his traveling companion and dear friend for Mark.

Barnabas wanted to take John Mark on the next trip, but Paul said, "No deal." Mark had quit before the real work had even begun on their first trip, and Paul did not want a quitter along (Acts 13:13; 15:38). He felt that Mark already had been given a chance and had bombed out.

Barnabas felt that Mark deserved another chance. He felt that people mature at different rates. Perhaps Mark had gotten involved over his head last time. He felt Mark was ready this time.

Barnabas could see Mark's potential and, rather than leave him undeveloped, separated from Paul for his next journey. He took Mark with him to Cyprus (15:39). We do not know the details of that trip, but we do know the results. Mark grew and glistened as a worker for God.

Mark later became Peter's traveling companion and translated Peter's sermons into other languages. He later teamed up with Paul (Colossians 4:10); he became one of those people whom Paul longed to see during his last stay in prison (2 Timothy 4:11). Barnabas was right again!

Barnabas' Example For Us

We do not know what kind of spiritual baby Barnabas was, but we certainly have a good idea of what a spiritual giant he was as a mature Christian. He did not just encourage with nice words. He got personally involved in the life of another.

His actions spoke much louder than his words. He sold property and gave money. He went before the apostles and pleaded for Paul. He went to Antioch and lived with the people. He sought Paul out and installed him in his first ministry. He took food to Jerusalem to relieve the christians there during a famine (Acts 11:29, 30). He gave Mark another chance to prove himself. He poured his faith into people. He put his ideas into practice; he put legs onto his thoughts. Neither the twelve apostles nor Paul could discourage him from encouraging another.

But Barnabas was not perfect. On one occasion, he did not see the best in others; he was down on the Gentiles (Galatians 2:11-13). This reminds us that the best and most mature of us can falter and make mistakes, but we don't give up and throw in the towel. Barnabas did not let that one negative episode dominate the rest of his life and ruin his effectiveness for the Lord. Nor did the people hang that episode over his head.

Barnabas never permitted a person's past to determine what that person could do or how he could be used in God's work. How often we restrict a person to his past failures! It is as if we were putting him into a straitjacket.

God always has accepted and used people who have goofed in the past. He does not want us to be chained to our failures. He wants us to learn and grow from our failures. He takes the ugly, broken pieces of our yesterdays and forms them into a beautiful mosaic for today and for all the tomorrows that follow. He did that with Jacob, Judah, Abraham, David, and Rahab; and He will do that for us today.

It is not that God is blind to our blunders. He simply looks over them to see the mature beings we can become. In this same way, Barnabas had hit God's target of being like Jesus. He could look beyond the muck to see the shining potential.

As you, too, are seeking maturity in Christ, consider acquiring "Barnabas" characteristics. Get involved with others and encourage them. Look for the potential in others. Look for the good in others, not the bad. Very possibly there is a "Paul" or a "Mark" who needs you. There is a church like Antioch who needs you. Keep a postiive outlook. Look around in church Sunday. You may be surprised what you can see with your blinders off!

Ananias

Volunteers for Jesus

Ananias

"Lie low, Christians." No doubt that was the word that had reached Damascus long before Saul got there. "Saul is on his way. Stay out of sight." Ananias would have been at the top of Saul's list, for he was known by all the Jews in the area (Acts 22:12).

Ananias was eager to do the bidding of God. All God had to do was call him by name, and Ananias immediately stood up to volunteer: "Behold, here am I, Lord" (Acts 9:10). We all know people like that. "We need a volunteer," and up go their hands.

Have you ever volunteered to go house to house, calling for the church? Then you know how scary that can be, don't you? There is always that bit of apprehension just before ringing the doorbell. Will they be home? What kind of people are they? What do they think of the church?

Ananias did not have that problem. His assignment card was filled with information about the prospect. He knew his prospect's name, address, and his background. The prospect was not the owner of the house on Straight Street, but was staying with someone else. His hometown was Tarsus. Now, that was enough right there to call it off. This man was an itinerant! Not even a citizen of the city! Even if he did respond, he would not become a functioning member of the congregation. It would be like bringing a new member in the front door, and watching him go out the back.

There are a lot of people like that in our communities. Who ever said that we are to witness to only those who are permanent residents? Are we really sensitive to the visitors in our services or in our communities? What about the traveling salesmen, the truck drivers, the construction workers, the migrant workers? What about those who go south for the winter and north for the summer? Is it a waste of time to call on them?

I wonder how many of the highly mobile people are hungering for someone to talk to them about the security that lies in God through Jesus. How many are in motel rooms ready for a witness, after watching a religious program on television, or after reading through some of the Gideon Bible, or after realizing how lonely they are?

Ananias' Doubts

It was obvious that God had been working before He gave Ananias his assignment to call on Paul. How do we know but that God has also been working ahead of time on that person who is our calling assignment? How many times have we decided not to go calling on a person because of his past?

Some of us might say, "I would go to that person if I had a direct message from God to do so, and the person was praying and waiting for me to come." But don't be so sure that the reluctance would be softened even then. Ananias got just that kind of message, "For behold, he is praying, and he has seen in a vision a man named Ananias come in and lay his hands on him, so that he might regain his sight" (9:11, 12). What a motivation! The man was waiting for him, knew his name, and what he was going to do. And yet Ananias was reluctant because of the *name* of the man on whom he was to call. It would be the same feeling we would get if we were assigned to call on a leader in the Mafia or on Mrs. Madalyn Murray O'Hair. How would we feel if we were told to call on the person in the community who was the most vocal and violent against Christianity? How eager would we be to go to the person who has been called on during revival meeting time for the past fifteen years? All the other callers had the door slammed in their faces. How enthusiastic would we be if the other callers reported hearing the shotgun go off as they backed out of the drive?

Saul was to Christianity what Hitler was to Judaism. Didn't God know that? "I volunteered, God, but let's talk this over," Ananias probably thought. "Just because Paul had received a vision about my coming does not mean he is going to be friendly. After all, he has been trying to get a look at me for some time. I know You are busy, God; maybe You overlooked some details." So Ananias gave God the news. "Lord, I have heard from many about this man, how much harm he did to Thy saints at Jerusalem; and here he has authority from the chief priests to bind all who call upon Thy name" (9:13, 14).

I certainly can understand Ananias' nervousness, can't you? Haven't you ever caught yourself filling God in on the details as if He had overlooked them? Ananias was not just making conversation; he was trying to convince God to change His mind! He just could not understand going to Saul. All his logic told him to avoid Saul.

But God said, "Go." Ananias needed to grow up and realize that God's way is not always man's way. God declared it long ago, "For as the heavens are higher than the earth, so are My ways higher than your ways" (Isaiah 55:9). When individuals take that seriously and become obedient servants, God can do fantastic things on this earth.

When Ananias understood that God truly wanted him to go to Saul, he was willing. God was patient with him, as He is with us when we react similarly. It was a super-tough assignment. There must have been several others he would rather have received, but he did as he was commanded. "And Ananias departed and entered the house—'' (Acts 9:17). Saul, who now began using his Greek name, Paul, appreciated his action. Years later, when he spoke before a mass of accusers, he gave to Ananias the credit that he deserved (22:1-16).

His Boldness

We can marvel at Ananias' boldness. He walked up to Saul and said, "Brother Saul—'' What? He called him *brother?* After he had gotten over his doubts, he was confident about what God was going to do and may have called him "brother" in anticipation of that (v. 13); or he may have just acknowledged that Paul and he were fellow Jews.

Without batting an eyelid, Ananias told Saul what to do. He immediately got to the point: "Why do you delay? Arise, and be baptized, and wash away your sins, calling on His name" (v. 16). Paul obeyed, recognizing that these instructions spoken by Ananias were significant words from God (9:18; Romans 6; 1 Corinthians 12:13; Galatians 3:26-28; Ephesians 4:5; Colossians 2:11, 12).

Ananias had to face the assignment of calling on an active antagonist, but he talked it over with God and matured in his thinking. He walked through the door of opportunity, and because of his boldness there was peace for Christians "throughout all Judea and Galilee and Samaria." It was a peace that allowed the church to be built up in stature and in numbers (Acts 9:31).

Just think how the tide of Christianity would have changed if Ananias had succumbed to his childish feelings and turned in his prospect card!

Stephen

Another type of bold witnessing is speaking the truth before an audience when you know the audience will be antagonistic. Stephen faced such an audience. He knew it was unpopular to suggest that God was not partial to a particular land, people, and building, as the Jews always had believed. But Stephen decided to speak what was true, instead of what was popular (Acts 7).

His message in that mass meeting cost him his life, but it gained him eternity. He was not accepted by his audience, but he was accepted by the angels of God. His speech was the pivotal point in the history of the spread of Christianity in the book of Acts.

I wonder, how many of us can be "Stephens" today or even be the type of audience that can accept a "Stephen"? There are many truths that need to be spoken, and these are unpopular with certain audiences: repentance before baptism, the mode of baptism, the necessity of baptism, equality of all races before God, and anyone that has put on Christ is a Christian despite what his group affiliation is, etc. We need to speak out on these issues, not just to our friends in private, but before the masses.

Perhaps this is the way the church will grow and spread like fire, as it did after the speech of Stephen in the first century (Acts 8:1 ff). It takes courage to speak out for the truth when the majority would not vote that way. It takes a mature man or woman of Christ.

These two men exemplify the boldness and willingness of mature Christians. They make footsteps that are tough to follow, but we must follow them, if we expect and hope for the growth of the church.

Paul

The Imitator

Are you able to admit it when you are wrong, even about your religion? Would you be willing to go down, way down, in the estimation of your family and friends for your religious beliefs? Could you put aside the religious teaching you received as a child?

Changing our religious positions is not easy, is it? The longer we have held a certain belief, the higher we get in positions of leadership in a certain church, the more difficult it is to change. How easy is it for an elder, a Sunday-school teacher, a preacher, or a Bible college teacher to take a look at his or her beliefs, to change positions, or even change a church affiliation? When our beliefs are challenged, we immediately defend our position as right and the other as wrong.

Just for a moment, let us examine our beliefs and our reasons for being part of a certain church. Did you choose your religion and church, or did someone else choose it for you? Were your parents affiliated with this church? Why? Were their people also a part of it? Do you feel, "If it was good enough for them, it is good enough for me"? Or do you say, "If I changed, I will be as much as saying that my parents are going to Hell"?

Is this church the nearest to you geographically, and the easiest for you to attend? Do you attend because you like the social group that is provided, because of the educational program for the children, or because it is the largest church in the community? Do you attend there because its size is the most like the one you attended as a child? Do you attend because

67

you agree with the teaching, or because you like the preacher?

Paul, Before Christ

Paul had to face such questions and the pain of examining his beliefs as he listened to the preaching of the converted Jews. He was determined to wipe out such teaching! He was not determined because of his own interests, but because of what he believed were God's interests. He was convinced that it was God's will that he oppose that Christian group.

Paul was "zealous for God" (Acts 22:3), and it was his zeal for God that made him think that he must "do many things hostile to the name of Jesus of Nazareth" (26:9). He was a fulfillment of Jesus' prediction that there would be opponents who would seek to kick Christians out of the synagogues and kill them, while thinking they were doing it as a service to God (John 16:2).

Paul was at the top of the ladder in the Judaistic religion (Philippians 3:4-6). When he walked in, everyone looked up. Even his scholarly teacher, Gamaliel (Acts 22:3), must have yielded the floor when Paul wished to speak. Paul had no equal (Galatians 1:14). But his advance in Judaism was not due to the superficiality of a sparkling personality nor to the philosophy of "I'll scratch your back if you scratch mine." Politicking was not a part of Paul's life. He did not sleep through Gamaliel's lectures and then drop Gamaliel's name from time to time in the right circles. His advance was a result of his commitment.

Paul did not gain renown because he challenged the status quo or kept coming up with new ideas. He ruffled no feathers. In fact, he was just the opposite of a "wave-maker." He admitted that he was "extremely zealous for my ancestral traditions" (v. 14). He was tradition-bound from his youth up, and all Jews knew that about him (Acts 26:4).

Paul traveled from synagogue to synagogue and

from city to city to get the Christians. His tactics were not mild either. He used physical force to get Christians to deny that Jesus was the Messiah. He tortured them and imprisoned them. When they would not budge, he saw to it that they were killed (Acts 22:4; 26:10, 11). He himself confessed that he was "furiously enraged at them" (26:11). He did all this, thinking that he was doing God a favor.

The New Birth

When Paul met Christ and discovered that his ideas and actions were not doing God a service, he changed. The persecutor became the persecuted. The same people that he formerly stood against, saying, "Get those Christians," he stood with saying, "Join these Christians."

Paul had been dedicated to serve God, not himself. He had decided that long before he took off for Damascus. What happened on that road did not change Paul's decision to be zealous for God. That kind of commitment did not change. What changed were Paul's ideas about what he thought was the truth. What he had thought was wrong, he then saw was right. He was committed to stand up for the truth because God is the author of truth.

When Jesus confronted Paul with the truth that He was indeed alive as the Christians had been teaching, Paul, the persecutor of the church, became a preacher for the church.

Can you imagine the humiliation Paul had to face from his former classmates at the Jerusalem Bible college? He had been at the top of the class; now he was not even a leader in the synagogue. What would he say to the "biggies" who gave him special letters of authority to arrest the Christians (Acts 9:2; 22:5)? He must have used his best logic and proof-texted the Old Testament to convince the authorities that the Christians needed to be silenced. How would he be able to say, "I used those Scriptures wrongly"? How would he face those who traveled with him and believed in his mission? He dumped them in Damascus. Their leader had quit them.

It takes a big man to begin standing *for* a position he had earlier stood *against*. Paul didn't even balk when he was commanded to be baptized (Acts 22:16). Such a practice was not compatible with the religion of his youth, but he was baptized, even though it went against all his religious training.

It is easy for some of us to be in a religion and decide that is where we will stay for the rest of our lives, without really evaluating our beliefs. "Not me," you say? Let's investigate more closely. How much time do you spend reading the Word of God? What topics have you studied lately? Have you *ever* really studied everything the Bible says about repentance, the Holy Spirit, baptism, grace, forgiveness, being lost, falling away from faith, elders, deacons, etc.? If not, why not?

"Not enough time," you say? You have got to be kidding! Americans have all kinds of time on their hands. That is why television is such a success—it requires time. That is why automobiles, "tour packages," and campers are sold so heavily. Leisure time is available.

Do you have enough courage to ask questions about the Scriptures you do not understand? Do you have enough determination to seek counsel that will help dispel some of your doubts? Are you open-minded enough to accept teaching that may be against what you learned as a child?

Growing Toward Christ's Character

He who sought to eradicate Christ became the imitator of Christ. He grew in many different aspects, seeking to be like Christ in his thoughts, attitudes, and actions.

Paul was formerly a Pharisee who harbored racial prejudices, but he taught that there should be no prej-

70

udices among Christians (Galatians 3:28). He taught that in order to win people to Christ, we must be willing to associate with different kinds of people. When he was with Gentiles, he observed their customs (1 Corinthians 9:19-23).

We like to say that association means assimilation; to cooperate with someone means we agree with all that he says. But when we are faced with the examples of Jesus and Paul, we cannot honestly concur with that statement. Could you ever worship on Saturday with a Seventh-Day Adventist? Would you ever participate in a foot-washing service? Would you ever observe the Lord's Supper with a different church group? Would you stop using the musical instrument when a noninstrumentalist worshiped with you? Paul would.

How quickly do we kick someone out of God's family when he or she makes a mistake? Paul wrote to a congregation that was divided over personalities, allowed sexual immorality, sued fellow members in the law courts, fussed and fought about what kinds of food to eat and what spiritual gifts to display, and even taught that life after death was doubtful. Yet he called that group of people a "church of God" (1 Corinthians 1:2).

I do not mean that he believed in "peace at all costs." He never covered up an error for the sake of harmony. He knew how to tell Peter he was all wet (Galatians 2:11). He knew when to suggest that it was time to disfellowship someone from the church (1 Corinthians 5; 1 Timothy 1:20). He knew when to tell the churches to straighten up, but he always did it for the good of the churches, not for his own good.

Do we have hang-ups about certain names for our churches? Paul didn't. He called God's people saints (Romans 1:7), the church (16:1), the church, or assembly, of God (1 Corinthians 1:2), the churches of Christ (Romans 16:16), the churches of the Gentiles (16:4), the churches of the saints (1 Corinthians

14:33), the church of the living God (1 Timothy 3:15), and faithful brethren (Colossians 1:2). Disciples were called Christians for the first time in Antioch where Paul was serving (Acts 11:26), but Paul himself never used that word to describe Christ's people or ever suggested that it would be the only designation that could be used. Are we imitating Paul, who was imitating Christ?

Paul maintained a balance between evangelism and edification. Nearly everywhere he spent a few days, he started a church. He was definitely *for* the church. He called the church the bride of Christ, the body of Christ, the temple of God, and the family of God. You never would have heard him bad-mouthing the church. He lived for what Christ died for—the church. He saw the church as God's mission on earth, and daily expressed concern for the church (2 Corinthians 11:28). He not only started new churches, but he also dedicated his energies to helping new Christians mature in Christ (Colossians 1:28). He wanted to see spiritual babies grow. In every letter he wrote, he urged people to grow.

Paul also believed in benevolence. He spent a great deal of his time collecting and taking food to hungry people (Acts 11:27-30; Romans 15:25-27; 1 Corinthians 16:1-4).

Paul was an apostle, but his attitude was not one of arrogance. He did not demand his "rights." He understood that God had called him to serve people, not to lord it over them. He wrote that God gave him authority for building people up, not tearing them down (2 Corinthians 13:10). That was exactly how he lived. He was willing to spend and be spent for the souls of mankind (12:15).

Paul knew that to bite and devour one another was to destroy one another (Galatians 5:15), and that to destroy one another would be to destroy the temple of God (1 Corinthians 3:16-19). He saw that the church could grow only as the members of Christ's body mutually honored one another (Romans 12:10), agreed with one another (12:16), loved one another (13:8), edified one another (14:19), were like-minded (15:5), received one another (v. 7), admonished one another (v. 14), greeted one another (16:16), waited for one another (1 Corinthians 11:33), cared for one another (12:25), served one another (Galatians 5:13), bore one another's burdens (6:2), put up with one another (Ephesians 4:2), spoke the truth (4:25), were kind to one another (v. 32), submitted to one another (5:21), forgave one another (Colossians 3:13), comforted one another (1 Thessalonians 4:18), and taught one another (Colossians 3:16).

Paul wrote *against* lusting for one another (Romans 1:27), judging one another (14:13), talking against one another (Galatians 5:15), irritating, challenging, and envying one another (5:26), lying to one another (Colossians 3:9), hating one another (Titus 3:3), and suing one another (1 Corinthians 1-6).

Paul was no lone-ranger Christian. He knew that Christians need one another just as much as they need Christ. He did not just go off and do "his own thing." He was a part of a team; he worked in cooperation with others. He worked side by side with Barnabas, Silas, Timothy, Titus, and others. They were not like him in every way; they had their own individualities. Paul did not try to make them like him or try to be independent of them.

Paul was a man who could be content with both abundance and poverty (Philippians 4:12), because he lived for others, not for himself. He could work at menial tasks for financial support (1 Corinthians 4:12), could receive financial support from churches (Philippians 4:15, 16; 2 Corinthians 11:8), and evidently could allow his associates to help him financially (Acts 18:1-5). He would not allow his "rights" to get in the way of his responsibilities. When others were weak, Paul felt it. When others were led to sin, he was intently concerned (2 Corinthians 11:29).

How Did He Do It?

"Oh, come on now! How could one man be all those things? Paul sounds like Mr. Super-Christian! He must have been a great egotist, or else it was all superficial! No? Then what was his secret?"

It is no secret. Paul tells us, "I am an imitator of Christ" (1 Corinthians 11:1).* He was no egotist. He gave up his popularity and status to become as scum in the eyes of men (Philippians 3:3-8; 1 Corinthians 4:13). No man would give these up for a superficial faith. He went from superficial pomp to supernatural power.

That same power is available to us. It is the power of Jesus' indwelling Spirit. That Spirit produces the character of Jesus in us (Galatians 5:22 ff; 2 Corinthians 3:18). To tap that power, we must be willing to change. We must be willing to cut loose from any past traditions that hinder us. We must be willing and determined to grow and advance as Paul did. We must forget about our "rights" and our own wishes; we must think about and care for others. Are you tapping that power? The evidence will be seen in how you are living and in what you are teaching.

As the life of Paul is studied in this lesson, we realize that we have barely scratched the surface of the character of this great man of God! He did not live to show off himself or his ideas. This was his philosophy: "I have been crucified with Christ; and it is no longer I who live, but Christ lives in me" (Galatians 2:20). He was saying, "Paul and his selfish interests were put to death; now Christ lives in here!"

How hard does Christ have to look to see himself within you? How long does He have to listen to hear himself within you?

Christ is saying, "Knofel, I see *you,* but where am *I?* I hear *you* talking, but where is *my* voice?"

Married, but Alone

"That poor child! He doesn't have much of a chance in this world. His parents did not consider what his problems would be if they got married. How could they even consider having a biracial baby?" This would have been the view of some when Timothy, a biracial baby, was born. Not much different from what we would say today, is it?

Timothy's mother was a Jew and his father was a Greek (Acts 16:1). In the eyes of many, that was an unacceptable mixture in the first century. It was even more unacceptable than a black/white marriage is in some circles today.

The Jews were reared to believe that Gentiles were not fully human. In some Jewish circles, Gentiles were considered more animal than human. They were called "dogs" and "pigs." In one instance, Jesus used the term "dogs" to refer to the Gentiles (Mark 7:27). Calling people "dogs" usually was intended as a put-down, although Jesus did not use it this way.

One of the most descriptive pictures of the worst desolation in the Old Testament was to die and be eaten by dogs (1 Kings 16:4; 21:19, 23). Stubborn and rebellious people were called "dogs" (Isaiah 56:10, 11; Matthew 7:6; Phillippians 3:2). Pagans who have no place in Heaven were referred to as "dogs" (Revelation 22:15).

For a Jew to marry a "dog" was absolutely terrible in the eyes of most people. The Jews could turn to verse after verse in the Scriptures to prove that Jews should not intermarry with Gentiles; and, of course

Eunice

the biracial children would be stigmatized all of their lives.

Such a child was Timothy. When we first read of him, we him, we are reminded that the Jews "all knew that his father was a Greek" (Acts 16:3). Not only was his father a Greek, but he was also a nonbeliever in the Jewish God. He did not participate in the Jewish religion. By this time in the first century, several Gentiles had become "God-fearers." They believed in the God of Abraham, Isaac, and Jacob, and had become proselytes to Judaism (Acts 2:10; 13:43).

Not Timothy's father. He would have nothing to do with that stuff. Probably he never darkened the door of the synagogue. I suspect he reacted bitterly to the way the Jews looked down upon his marriage. We are sure about his "hands off" policy toward the Jewish religion, because he did not allow Timothy to be circumcised. What teaching Timothy received about God came from his mother, not his father.

The Faithful Mother

What possible good could come from a biracial boy who had no example or teaching from his father concerning morality or religion? He must have had a mother who never gave up. In spite of her husband's refusal to believe, she never gave up her faith. She taught her son about her faith and was a good example for him (2 Timothy 1:5).

A mother who takes her family to the church services without her husband has such a lonely feeling. She is uncomfortable. Once when I spoke to a church gathering, I mentioned how uncomfortable many unmarried adults are in the services. A woman from the audience spoke to me afterward, making this observation: "Married women who come alone are also uncomfortable."

It would be tempting for the woman to give up and say, "The man is to be the head of the family. If he won't lead out in this area of our lives, I won't either. I don't want to go to the worship services unless we go together. I'll wait until he is ready." In such a case, while she waits the children grow older and older and have no spiritual guidance.

Little children need before them an example of faith in God and Jesus. They need someone to go with them to the services, not just leave them. They need someone to see them take part in the special programs. They need someone there when they sing for the first time in the choir. They need someone to sing "Jesus Loves Me" and "The B-I-B-L-E" with them. They need someone to tuck them in at night with a prayer. They need someone to take them to the youth meetings, encourage them to go to camp, and introduce them to Christian colleges, Bible Bowls, and youth conventions. They not only need a youth minister at the church, they also need one at home.

"But isn't the wife supposed to submit to her husband in *everything*? If he does not live the faith, should I? If he wants to stay home Sunday mornings, shouldn't I?" These are becoming popular questions in church circles today. Some people advise that the wives should stay home with the husbands, but I question that advice.

Eunice kept her faith and lived it, although her husband did not share that part of life with her. I think we also have a clear teaching on this matter from Peter in Acts 5. A husband, Ananias, decided with his wife's knowledge to try to deceive the church (vv. 1, 2). Probably he wanted to get some of the praise that was given to Barnabas, by pretending to do what Barnabas had done (4:36, 37).

Ananias' scheme did not work. Peter confronted not only Ananias about the deception, but also his wife, Sapphira. He asked a question that criticized her action, "Why is it that you have agreed *together?*" (Acts 5:9). The point is that Sapphira should not have gone along with her husband's scheme.

Peter taught on this same issue, concerning a wife

78

living with an unbelieving husband. He spoke about the powerful influence of a believing wife's behavior with her unbelieving husband (1 Peter 3:1-6). Just as a faithful "Eunice" can produce a "Timothy," she also can gently lead her husband to the Lord. Even though she and her husband are not united in the Lord, she lives with him with gentleness and goodness. She submits to him by living unselfishly. She does not preach to him or nag him (3:1).

But just because the wife does not "push" her faith does not mean she compromises that faith. She expresses her faith through her life and this can be more effective than words. Men don't like to be told what to do. She expresses her faith in the "quality of a gentle and quiet spirit." She doesn't ignore him because he ignores her Lord. Men like to be noticed and respected; she meets his needs. Her reaction to her husband's unbelief should not be a personal war she is waging. The only conflict should be in his reaction to Christ that shines through her life, not a face-to-face confrontation.

The wife should not hide the fruit of the Spirit just because the husband does not like or cannot accept that kind of life-style. If he doesn't, he has the right to decide not to stay around (1 Corinthians 7:12-15). But the wife should not change her "colors" under the guise of submission. If that is what Paul meant by submission, his advice in 1 Corinthians 7 would not make sense.

Much of what has been said so far is hard for some people to swallow. The next statements will be just as difficult for some of you to believe. A wife and mother is to be dedicated to making her contribution to society primarily by the quality of life she pours into her homemaking responsibilities.

From books, movies, television, newspaper columns, seminars, interviews, etc., women are told that homemaking is a waste of their womanhood. A woman is programmed into thinking that she will be bored, unfulfilled, frustrated, and she will become dull, dumb, and hemmed in if she does not cut away from the homemaking drudgery.

My wife, Julia, is a great homemaker; she is a fulfilled woman. If she evaluated her daily responsibilities as merely sweeping floors, fixing meals, and washing dirty clothes, she could possibly buy the popular theme that homemaking is restrictive. Instead, she feels that any major activity outside the home to which she *had* to devote eight hours a day would restrict her creativity and diversity.

At home with a husband and four children, Julia is an administrator, a teacher, a judge sometimes, and a lawyer at other times. She is a chauffeur, an interior decorator, a nurse who diagnoses and prescribes medicine. She is both an "Emergency 51" and a "Rampart" hospital. She is a television and movie censor. She is a director and author of dramatic plays. She is a model who is idolized by her fans. She is a writer and editor. She is the head of consumers' interests, always checking products and prices.

Julia is an avid reader, keeping up on current world affairs. Since she is involved in church work and helping others, she is not isolated. Her goal is to boost her husband in his work and to help her children become like Christ. She is a "Eunice" and is not embarrassed by it.

Ladies, don't ever regret being a "Eunice." Without Eunices we would have few young preachers like Timothy. Paul worked with Timothy and depended upon him to a great degree. But even Paul recognized that he could not appreciate Timothy without also appreciating the faith of his mother, Eunice. That faith had everything to do with Timothy's effectiveness in his ministry.

Mothers, don't ever give up, even if you don't have a partner, or if you are without a believing one. Be an example continuously to your children. They need you. The future of the world is depending on you.

A Loving Grandmother

Neither could Paul forget Timothy's grandmother, Lois (2 Timothy 1:5). The importance and power of grandparents in the lives of children cannot be overemphasized.

Society has done a devastating thing in this country. The age groups are separated far too much. We have developed what one man calls a split-level society. The aged are shelved, and many people feel that senior citizens are useless. We are one of the few cultures that have done this. In this area, I think we need to return to a more primitive way of thinking and acting toward our elderly.

In many other cultures, it is taught that the older a person becomes the more beneficial he or she is to the community. I personally believe that. Older people, on the whole, have much wisdom and maturity. They have so much to share.

A person who regularly works with prison inmates observed that a grandmother has more influence with a prisoner than anyone else. It was discovered on the east coast that the people who had the most success counseling with drug addicts were not the professional counselors, but the grandparents.

A recent research team discovered that the majority of juvenile delinquents never had a functioning grandparent in their growing-up days. We are discovering that grandparents pour into the lives of children much of the stability, security, and direction that they need.

I can testify to that in our own family. I can still hear my grandmother Crane laugh, and I can still taste her homemade bread. I will always remember her faith. Even when she was in her eighties, she never missed Bible school and church. Much of her goodness was due to her godliness, and I could see that even as a small boy. She never had much materially. In fact, when she died, the welfare department took all the property she had.

But my grandmother gave one thing that I never could have saved enough money to buy: her time and attention. I am convinced that the money we spend on our children and grandchildren does not really impress them. Maybe it impresses us or our friends, but not the children. What does impress the children? The time we invest in them, and grandparents usually have a lot of that to spare.

Be a functioning grandparent! Our children's grandparents are great. My mother remembers every special occasion, even Valentine's Day. She sends the children postcards when she is on a trip. She wants to know when they lose a tooth so she can send a nickel or a dime in the next letter. My wife's mother always brings them some little toy when she comes to see them. She is always willing to read a book to them. It is no wonder that nothing excites our children more than a trip to see their grandparents.

Don't spoil the grandchildren, though. Give them some direction in their lives. Our children usually spend a week or so with each set of grandparents during the summer. Several weeks after one of these visits, I noticed that Randy's table manners had improved. I had nagged him about them for quite some time. I was pleasantly surprised and asked, "Why did you begin doing that?" "Grandmother told me to do it," he replied. I had tried to get him to improve, but my words had gone in one ear and out the other. But when grandmother told him to do so, it was done!

I imagine Timothy talked to Paul about his grandmother many times while traveling and when Paul was in prison. His grandmother's faith had left its mark on him, and Paul could see it.

I don't suppose anyone has as much influence on children as do their grandparents. Be aware of that influence and use it wisely. When you may be forgetful, you can be sure that you will be remembered by your grandchildren. Something of you lives on in the lives of your grandchildren.

Lois With Timothy

You don't even have to have children of your own or grandchildren of your own to be a functioning grandparent. The "grandparent age" is enough to qualify you. No one who visits our home is enjoyed more by our children than grandparent-type people. Our children identify with them immediately and are on their laps cuddling with them before we know it. Why not look around for some children who have no grandparents and "adopt" them? Share your faith, your wisdom, and your time with them. Remember their birthdays and do special things with them.

In Medicine Lodge, Kansas, recently, I met one of the most influential "grandfathers" I have ever met. He was in his sixties, a farmer, and had never married. He had no child, but he had more "adopted grandchildren" than anyone I know. He carried pictures of all his grandchildren in his wallet—he had scores of them. He knew the children by name, age, and their special characteristics. He writes them all regularly and remembers them on birrthdays and Christmas. Everyone in the church talks about his love and influence with the children. What a grandparent!

Conclusion

We do not have much information about Eunice and Lois, but we can see the results of their lives in Timothy. From Paul's remarks we can surmise the type of women they were. When Paul saw Timothy, he saw the shadows of his mother and grandmother.

Don't feel sorry for yourself if you are rearing a child alone, or if you have an unbelieving partner, or if you are the grandparent in a racially or religiously mixed family. Remember Eunice and Lois. Stand tall and faithful. Show forth the gentle and quiet spirit. Show by your example what it means to be like Jesus. It is not easy, but it is always triumphant!

The Peacemaker

Christians need one another. A classic example of this truth is the relationship between Paul and Timothy. We cannot understand Timothy until first we understand his relationship with Paul. Timothy needed Paul to teach him, to encourage him, to point out his abilities to him. Paul needed Timothy to augment his own ministry. They were members of the church, the body of Christ, and they belonged to one another (Romans 12:5).

Although Christians are connected to the head, Christ, we are held together, supported, and maintained by the other members to whom we also belong. God has so designed the church so our needs can be met through our contact with other Christians (Ephesians 4:16; Colossians 2:19).

In order for God's design to be accomplished, each person must consider others as important as himself (Romans 12:3). Each must be devoted to the other, not just to himself (12:10). Each must give preference to the other. Neither must brag in arrogance about how much more gifted he is than his teammate (1 Corinthians 12:21; 13:4). There is no room for jealousy or feelings of inferiority (12:15). No one should try to make another become just like himself. The members must allow their many differences to complement each other and build up each other in the faith (Romans 12:6; 1 Corinthians 12:7; 14:12).

I'm afraid Christians today have been slow to accept these principles and put them into practice in our lives. Sometimes our churches, who have many ministers on the same staff, violate the Biblical pattern of teamwork. Often one of the ministers acts like the "top dog" and runs the whole show. Sometimes one will delegate to another member of the staff only those jobs that will keep him out of the spotlight. Sometimes one of the ministers will become more popular with the people, making one of the others jealous. Sometimes one of the ministers will seem to slip and fall, but he will receive no help from others on the team. Paul and Timothy's relationship did not have any of these characteristics. We can learn so much from their ministries to each other and to the church at large.

The Paul-Timothy Team

Paul had the "right" to be called the senior minister. He was older, more experienced, and he made Timothy, who was a biracial nobody, into a somebody. Timothy became so well known that Paul often included Timothy's name when he wrote to a congregation (2 Corinthians 1:1; Philippians 1:1; Colossians 1:1; 1 Thessalonians 1:1; 2 Thessalonians 1:1). Paul needed Timothy, as we will consider later, but Paul had every reason to call himself Number One.

He did refer to himself as Timothy's father in the faith (1 Corinthians 4:17; 1 Timothy 1:2, 18; 2 Timothy 1:2). He was not saying this as a put-down. He was simply expressing the very close relationship he and Timothy enjoyed. He coupled the father-son designation with other designations, such as: "fellow-worker" (Romans 16:21) and "brother" (2 Corinthians 1:1). They were, first and foremost, members of a team.

Timothy was a fantastic team member who did not try to undermine his teacher by talking behind his back, trying to steal his popularity, or taking his place in the work. He was not any kind of a threat to Paul; he was a servant to Paul. He loved to serve Paul as a son loves to serve a father (Philippians 2:22). That is not easy when the person you are serving is so popular and what you are doing is helping increase his popularity.

Timothy could have been called Paul's right-hand man, for he could see that Paul's was such an important ministry, and whatever he could do to help he would do. He didn't care who got the credit.

How do we know anything about Timothy then? Because Paul spoke of him so many times. You see, Paul lived out what he preached. He told the people to give preference to others, and he did that himself. Paul *wanted* people to know about Timothy's value. He didn't try to hide him out of fear that his own popularity would wane. He turned the spotlight on Timothy many times.

There is far too little appreciation being passed around within the family of God these days. A person can burn himself out in service without one nod of approval from his associates. Paul would not allow that to happen to Timothy. He called Timothy "beloved and faithful" (1 Corinthians 4:17). He said, "He is doing the Lord's work" (16:10). He referred to him as a "bond-servant of Jesus Christ" (Philippians 1:1). He wrote, "I have no one else of kindred spirit who will genuinely be concerned for your welfare" (2:20); "You know of his proven worth" (2:22). Wouldn't Paul have been a great employer?

Paul not only commended Timothy, he also protected him. Before he sent him to Corinth, Paul wrote to the congregation there and said, "See that he is with you without cause to be afraid . . . Let no one therefore despise him. But send him on his way in peace" (1 Corinthians 16:10, 11). Partially to protect Timothy from embarrassment, Paul had him circumcised (Acts 16:3). He wanted to free him from having to use any self-defense tactics. Paul did not have the philosophy, "Let him make his own way as I had to do." Instead, he shared the many things he had learned from experience.

Paul also equipped Timothy for the work. There

Timothy

were no vague assignments that left Timothy wondering what to do and how to do it, then feeling bad because he failed. Paul spelled out exactly what he was to do. Paul did not delegate just unimportant tasks to him. He knew that the best way to bring out a man's abilities was to give him important work to do, so he could have the satisfaction of a job well done. Paul gave Timothy tasks that were within his ability and interest.

Paul also included Timothy in any credit he received. He made it clear that Timothy preached Jesus in Corinth also (2 Corinthians 1:19). When Paul was living in his last days, he knew that Timothy was getting discouraged. So He took pen in hand and wrote him to motivate him to keep on, and the second letter to Timothy was born.

Do you have this type of relationship with those you work with? Husbands, wives, parents, children, employers, employees, and ministers can certainly learn a lot from the Paul-Timothy team.

Timothy, The Servant

Have you ever noticed how Paul often came into a city *walking,* but left the city *running?* He would come into a relatively peaceful atmosphere and leave with things pretty "shook up." Sometimes he came in good health, but left with wounds. Paul was the type of person who ruffled feathers easily. His ministry needed the balance of a person who had a different personality. Timothy was that person. He did not upset applecarts, as Paul tended to do.

I do not mean that Timothy ever compromised his faith. He believed just what Paul believed and cared for people as much as Paul did. But somehow even after Paul was kicked out of a city, Timothy could stay behind there. He would pick up the pieces and work a long time with some of the same people who had been turned off by Paul.

It was not long after Timothy joined Paul that Paul and Silas were put into prison, but Timothy was not (Acts 16:19). Why? Somehow Timothy never came across the same way that Paul did. People were not as threatened by him. He was more quiet and timid, but he was effective. Paul needed him.

After the Philippian uproar, the team went to Thessalonica. There it happened again. There was violent opposition against Paul and Silas, but Timothy was not mentioned, though he was there. Some of the brethren there even put up bond money, evidently to assure that Paul would not return (Acts 17:9). But guess who was allowed to come back? That's right! Timothy! (1 Thessalonians 3:2).

In the same places where there was opposition to Paul, there was none toward Timothy. In the letters he wrote to those places, Paul included Timothy's name in the greeting (Corinth, Philippi, Thessalonica). Timothy may have had a rapport with some of the people that Paul did not. He did strengthen their faith and encourage them after Paul left.

After Thessalonica, it happened again—

opposition against Paul. The Christians sent Paul on, but Timothy stayed in Berea (Acts 17:14). Paul was no lone ranger. He needed the rest of the team, so he sent for Silas and Timothy to come as soon as possible (Acts 17:15). What did "as soon as possible" mean? Surely not "drop everything and come immediately." He probably meant "come and join me as soon as the follow-up work in Berea is finished." What was the follow-up work? Evidently, it was the strengthening of the new Christians and the selection of leaders to carry on the work.

Paul had not been in Athens long before he became anxious about how the new Christians were doing in Thessalonica. Paul had spent only three weeks there and left the Christians in the midst of an opposing environment. He could not permit them to think "out of sight, out of mind." He had never read in the ministerial ethics books that once you leave a place, you forget about it. If he ever was taught that, he flunked the course. He sent to Thessalonica the one person who could go there and be accepted by all: Timothy (1 Thessalonians 3:1-8). One of Timothy's finest contributions to God's work was to go to cities that had been disturbed and work effectively and patiently with the brethren.

Paul was without funds when he got to Corinth. He started making tents for a living, but when Silas and Timothy came down from Macedonia, "Paul began devoting himself completely to the word, solemnly testifying to the Jews that Jesus was the Christ" (Acts 18:5). It may have been that Timothy went to work to support the team. Timothy knew by then that Paul needed him on the team. He could have questioned, "Me? Do menial labor? Not on your life!" But Timothy would have been a willing supporter of Paul's ministry as well as an ideal follow-up man.

What would happen today in a team ministry if funds were low? Would the "assistant" stick with the team even if he had to work in a factory to make ends meet, or would he look for another ministry? It would be tough. I would not want to be in that situation. Perhaps I don't have Timothy's attitude. Do you?

We must not assume that all Timothy did in Corinth was work to bring home the bacon. No, Paul would not have allowed his whole time to be spent doing that. Timothy also preached in Corinth (2 Corinthians 1:19) and was sent on special missions by Paul.

Not only was Timothy a follow-up man, he was also an advance man (Acts 19:22; 20:4, 5). Who would be better to send ahead to prepare the people for Paul's arrival, than someone who would work quietly in the background and yet not compromise his faith?

Where did Timothy get such a disposition and ability to keep the peace? Remember his home life and the examples of his mother and grandmother. He was accustomed to living in a mixed religious setting (see Acts 16). He learned to live in that environment without warfare and without compromise. Little did his mother know that her reactions to a difficult situation would be preparing Timothy for a his ministry.

We may think that what happens at home is just private, but it expands to the larger world through our children. To a great extent, how we as parents react to situations at home will be the way our children will react to situations in the outside world. That is why I feel it is important that we exercise good judgment about what our children watch on television and what type of literature they read. We do not want them to hear or read that our standards and values are not valid anymore. We do not want them to feel that they must meet opposition with violence. We do not want them to get the wrong view of life.

Timothy was also a trouble-shooter for Paul. He had the knack of sitting down with people who were at odds with one another, or who were at odds with

Paul, and bringing them together as brothers and sisters.

There was trouble brewing at Philippi. We cannot read Philippians without sensing that something was wrong inside the church. That was why Paul talked about such things as conducting themselves in a manner worthy of the gospel (Philippians 1:27); doing nothing from conceit, but looking out for others (2:3, 4); taking on a servant's attitude (2:5-11); doing things without grumbling (v. 14); receiving Epaphroditus with joy (vv. 25-30); helping the two women who were fussing (4:2, 3); remembering that he had not desired their financial help (vv. 10-20).

Why do you suppose Paul spent time talking about the financial help he had received from them, and the fact that he was sending Epaphroditus home early, while he was evangelizing even though in prison? I suspect that there was disunity in that church over whether or not to continue supporting Paul financially while he was in prison. Some thought, "If we are going to support someone, let's support one who is able to evangelize, not someone stuck in prison." Others thought, "The man we sent with the money is now coming home early. Our money has been wasted." So Paul not only wrote an explanation, and sent Epaphroditus back to fill them in on the details, but also sent Timothy. Timothy could evaluate a condition accurately and treat it properly.

Paul also sent Timothy as a trouble-shooter to Corinth in the midst of all their troubles (1 Corinthians 16:10). Paul had written several letters, trying to deal with their problems (5:9; 2 Corinthians 7:8). He had made at least one trip back to Corinth to discuss the problem (2 Corinthians 2:1), but things had not improved. Thus he sent Timothy. Timothy's ministry with those people was so successful that by the time Paul sent someone else to see how things were going, the problems were solved (7:5-16).

Even at the end of his life, Paul left Timothy at a

trouble spot (1 Timothy 1:3). Things had not been going well at Ephesus. Some Christians were becoming independent of the gospel and teaching false doctrine, and others were listening (1:3, 4). Some men were having independent attitudes about their governmental leaders (2:1-7). Some wives were trying to become independent of their husbands (2:9-15). Some people were trying to water down the qualifications of the elders to get their own men elected, that is, those who would agree with the false doctrine (3:1-7). Some were even wanting to select servants of the church who had questionable characters (vv. 8-13). Who could come into such an atmosphere and pull the people together around the common cause of Christ? Timothy!

For Us Today

Timothy was able to grow to maturity in Christ because of the examples of his mother and grandmother and because of the guidance and teaching of Paul. He was able to grow because fellow Christians helped him, and he was able in turn to help others to grow and mature spiritually.

I hope that we are trying our best to help our fellow Christians grow in Christ. Let us encourage and undergird them. When Paul was dying, he wrote to Timothy to urge him on and challenge him. How often have you written a letter to encourage someone who is burning himself or herself out for the church? Oh, you are too busy? Do you feel you should be receiving the "roses" instead of handing them out?

Paul wrote his letter when he was in prison and knew that his execution was just around the corner (2 Timothy 4:7, 8). But he did not want to die without lifting up the one who had served him as a son serves a father, the one who would work so he could preach, the one who would stay behind so he could go on, and the one who would go back and work through the knotty problems of Christians going through the pains of spiritual infancy. While Paul was all things to all people (1 Corinthians 9:20-23), Timothy was all things to Paul.

I wonder if you and I can become like that to another Christian brother or sister. Many times we find fault with the church and criticize the Sunday-school teacher, the preacher, the elders, or the people in the pews. Why don't we try to be more like Timothy and help those people fulfill their individual ministries? We could find ways to do it, if we tried hard enough.

If you are a leader in the church, are you treating your followers and fellow workers right? Are you help-ing them grow toward spiritual maturity and helping them use their special abilities to upbuild the work of the church? Here are some principles that Paul fol-lowed that would be well worth your time to consider, leader:

(1) Select your workers personally and convince them of their potential.

(2) Equip them to do the work.

(3) Protect them from possible misunderstanding and mistreatment.

(4) Associate with them closely.

(5) Teach them from your experience.

(6) Treat them as fellow workers, not subordi-nates.

(7) Give them encouragement and appreciation for their works.

(8) Build them up in front of others.

(9) Give people tasks that are in line with their abilities and interests.

(10) Be an example worthy of imitation.

All members of the team working for Christ need each other. They will all find fulfillment as they seek to practice in their lives what Jesus said, "If any one wants to be first, he shall be last of all, and servant of all" (Mark 9:35). That is what it means to be a part of the family of God, part of the church, which is the body of Christ.

Movers
For the Master

Move One

Only a homeowner who has poured himself into his home can appreciate the pain and discomfort of leaving his home and environment that is familiar to him. But Aquila and Priscilla were a married couple who considered their relationship to God as top priority. They were given the choice of leaving Rome or denouncing their faith (Acts 18:2). Instead of keeping their home and their place of business, and staying in familiar surroundings, they moved to Corinth.

Paul hadn't been in the city long before he heard about this couple and their active faith. He became their house guest and must have been their personal teacher (Acts 18:3). Wouldn't that have been a thrill?

Move Two

Aquila and Priscilla became so attached to Paul as a friend and teacher that when he left, they left. They didn't leave to play the "follow the preacher" game. No, they left to join Paul's ministerial team. They left to get involved in a new church work. Paul deposited them in Ephesus (Acts 18:18, 19). Aquila and Priscilla must have laid the groundwork for Paul's later ministry of three years in Ephesus (20:17, 31).

What a couple! Not only did they leave one place because of their faith, but they voluntarily left another place for their faith. They wanted to spread the faith to other locations, so they moved.

We live in a highly mobile society. One out of every five families moves to another location every year. Ask any group of people how many of them have moved during the past five years and more than half of them will raise their hands.

How do we express our faith in our moving? Is that even a consideration in any of our contemplations about moving? It is rather common for a family who was active in a small town, conservative church to "drop out" of religious activity when it moves to the city. Most of the Christians from southern Illinois who moved into the Chicago area cannot be found. They have vanished as far as any contact with a church is concerned. They kept up their connections with the grocery store, post office, the doctor, the dentist, the barber, and the beauty shop, but not the church.

Aquila

Don't blame the lack of growth of our churches all on the preachers. Some of it should go to those who moved and never set foot in a church again. President Carter observed that when you move your cook stove you should move your church membership.

Aquila and Priscilla moved, but that is not the last we hear of them. While they were in Ephesus, an expert Bible scholar came to town preaching and teaching. Apollos evidently was an intellectual giant, for he came from Alexandria, a city known for its fine colleges. He was like a Harvard graduate with a Ph.D. in religion. He was like a walking encyclopedia. His speech was eloquent (18:24).

Yet Apollos was not an intellectual snob who turned people off by his manner. He spoke on their level, and many people became his followers (1 Corinthians 1:12). He was no fake. He was fervent in spirit, not superficial. He had been "instructed in the way of

Priscilla

the Lord" and was "teaching accurately the things concerning Jesus" (Acts 18:25).

Aquila and Priscilla listened to Apollos, and they must have appreciated both his knowledge and his ability to communicate. They must have loved his enthusiasm and the things he taught about Jesus. They also noticed that he erred in one point of his teaching—baptism. Apollos was "acquainted only with the baptism of John" (18:25).

What would you have done about his error, just ignore it? I doubt it. We usually are only too ready to pounce on someone else's mistake, but not on a one-to-one basis with the person himself. No, the popular tendency is to start telling other people about his mistakes. We keep bringing it up until others won't listen to *anything* he has to say.

I know of preachers who were "run off" because of the friction that was caused by people who talked behind their backs so much that even their friends doubted them. *Anything* they said would be twisted to perpetuate the errors in doctrine they had. Bitterness followed, and the person whose teaching was wrong never was helped. In fact, the reactions were as erroneous as the original error in teaching.

Let us learn from Aquila and Priscilla in handling the situation. They did not publicly rebuke Apollos. They did not call their own meeting to denounce his teachings. They saw that he was accurate in what he taught *about Jesus.* They were not arrogant about their superior knowledge, or the fact that their teacher had been Paul.

It is easy to get puffed up about the preacher who taught us or about the school we attended. Aquila and Priscilla could have compared their school—the apostle Paul—to Apollos' fancy school at Alexandria, and said, "No wonder he is so wrong. Look where he got his schooling!"

It is sad how graduates of one school can look down their noses at graduates of another school. A teaching colleague of mine experienced that on a plane from Joplin to Los Angeles. He sat next to a man who was getting his Ph.D. in theology from an elite school. When he discovered that my friend had a Master of Divinity degree, he said, "That's not a teaching degree; why are you teaching?"

When Ken explained he was teaching at a Bible college, he said sarcastically, "Let's preach to the people in this plane. I'll preach to the first-class section—to the intellect, and you preach to the people in the coach—to their emotions." As Ken left him, he said, "May God bless you." The puffed-up intellectual replied, "Oh, He does!"

But Aquila and Priscilla did not look down their noses at Apollos. They did not even drop Paul's name, as far as we know. Instead, they took Apollos aside and "explained to him the way of God more accurately" (Acts 18:26). They probably brought him home to dinner and discussed the way of God. What a fine thing to do!

How many of our preachers would be greatly helped if some of the members in the church would simply take them aside privately and explain certain Bible passages to them? I wonder how many young men just out of the Bible college or seminary have quit early because the errors in their preaching were handled harshly by the church people.

Aquila and Priscilla were effective, not only because of their attitude, but also because of Apollos' attitude. Apollos was open-minded. He accepted further teaching. He did not close his ears to this couple just because he came from Alexandria. It takes a big person to admit when he is wrong. Aquila and Priscilla were able to nurture his faith because he was willing to change and grow.

Christianity spreads not because of how high our egos have become, but because of how high we hold up God's truth. Let us all be willing to be taught as well as to teach.

Move Three

This fine Christian couple moved again. This time they moved back to Rome. They had a church meeting in their home (Romans 16:3-5). They were not about to get lost in the big city. Isn't it interesting that two of the great letters in the New Testament were written to congregations that may have begun in their home?

We read a very significant verse in Romans: "—to whom not only do I give thanks, but also all the churches of the Gentiles" (16:4). Why is this verse significant? Because the first time we read about Aquila and Priscilla, they were being kicked out of Rome because they were Jews (Acts 18:1, 2). Then we read how grateful *Gentile* Christians were for them. They matured in Christ, for now, even though they were Jews, they had put aside their prejudices and evidently had an integrated congregation meeting in their home. This may be how they risked their lives for Paul.

Move Four

The last time we read about Aquila and Priscilla, they were back in Ephesus (2 Timothy 4:19). I suspect that they became aware of the tough problems that had developed in the Ephesian congregation, and moved back to be a stabilizing influence in the life of that church.

Conclusion

Every time this couple moved, they served the Master. In their tracks they left a powerful preacher (Apollos), a church in Ephesus, and a church in Rome.

What are we leaving in our tracks as we move about the country? For whom do we move? For whom do we live when the unpacking is finished?

Room for the Rich

It's calling night at the church. You have the prospect card in your hand. You don't recognize the name on the card, and there are no written details about the family. You hop in the car and drive to the address.

"Can this be right?" you wonder as you look down the winding drive lined with cedar trees. You catch your breath, and your eyes widen as you look upon the fifteen-room red brick mansion with the huge, white columns stretching up beside the front door. You notice the lavish lawn, the three-car garage with the Cadillac and the boat parked out front, the rose garden, the Olympic-sized pool, and the full-sized tennis court. Your first inclination is to turn around, stop at a cafe for a cup of coffee, and return to church with your prospect card marked "no response."

After all, how do you approach a rich person and speak to him about Jesus? With all their obvious success, how do you convince the rich that they need Jesus? Too long we have neglected them in our evangelistic efforts. We must realize that their need for God is just as real as anyone else's. Often the rich are lonely and empty. They are envied and hated by others. They are thought of only in terms of dollar signs. I think we would be amazed at how readily they would respond to a church or an individual who showed concern and care for them.

The Tax Man

Matthew was a rich tax gatherer. It is said that some men in his position made over $100,000 a year.

Matthew

When you remember that the average day's wage at that time was twenty cents, you can grasp how rich Matthew was. He was hated and envied because he got his riches out of the pockets of the people.

The Roman government would auction off the right to collect taxes. Only people with money in the first place could get such a job. Rome had had a tough time collecting the revenues, so she merely decided how much money she wanted and then told the collectors that they could keep any extra moneys for themselves. Many of the tax men took advantage of this overtaxing the people in order to fatten their own pockets.

The Jews hated these gatherers so much that they barred them from the synagogue, even though they were Jews. Robbers, murderers, and tax gatherers were classed together. Leviticus 20:5 was said to be talking about the tax collectors: "Then I Myself will set My face against that man and against his family;

and I will cut off from among their people both him and all those who play the harlot after him."

Jesus came for the lost. He did not hate Matthew. He asked him to become His disciple. The fishermen left their nets to follow Jesus, and Matthew left his money table to follow Him. He gave up his business and laid down his purse full of money, to take up a new life and a pen to write the truth about Jesus. He gave up taxing for Caesar in order to teach for Christ. Commitment is not reserved for the poor.

This rich man with the pen recorded the Sermon on the Mount, many of the best-known parables, and the Great Commission. He who was barred from the synagogue wrote his Gospel for the Jews, to convince them that Jesus was the true Messiah. No doubt Matthew talked to his rich friends about Jesus and the change brought about in his life because of Him. Perhaps this is how Zacchaeus heard of Jesus.

The Tree Climber

Zacchaeus was a chief tax collector, so it is possible that he was Matthew's boss at one time. He got a commission from all the collectors under him, and this made him wealthy (Luke 19:2). He was small physically, but he was big in courage.

Jesus was coming to town, and Zacchaeus did what you would think a ten-year-old boy would do. He shinnied up a tree to get a better look. If only there had been a television camera to pick up that stunt! The richest man in town was up a tree! Evidently, Zacchaeus did not care what others thought. He did not live to impress people, and he had a need for what Jesus had to offer.

There is nothing sophisticated about climbing a tree. Contrary to popular belief, the rich often have fewer hang-ups about doing lowly tasks than some middle-class folk. I visited a church last year in which a woman millionaire always served as a waitress at the church dinners. She did not plan or organize the dinners, she served them! The preacher told me that she and her husband would scrub floors, anything, to be of service.

Jesus knew Zacchaeus' name when He noticed the man in the tree. Jesus knew all things, and needed no introduction to people. This was true in the case of Nathanael (John 1:47-50). But I suspect that Jesus also may have heard several people mention the name of Zacchaeus as they pointed and snickered. Jesus saw that if humiliation did not bother Zacchaeus, he could be a dynamic disciple.

So Jesus, who did not own a pillow on which to lay His head, went home with the richest man in the area. Jesus was an example for us. He came to break down the barriers that divide us and keep us from being brothers. He wanted us to accept the poor *and* the rich.

Zacchaeus received Jesus gladly (Luke 19:6). He was not embarrassed by Jesus' carpenter background or His poverty-stricken family. Jesus changed Zacchaeus' life, and Zacchaeus declared his unselfishness, "Half of my possessions I will give to the poor" (Luke 19:8). That is quite a bit more than the ten percent that many Christians brag about. Be careful when criticizing the rich!

Zacchaeus started a new life and showed real repentance: "If I have defrauded anyone of anything, I will give back four times as much." That's something for a man who made his living cheating people! He met Jesus, started a new life, and grew toward becoming like Jesus.

Perhaps you don't think this relates to you, since you don't cheat people. Let's not be too quick to bury the application. Are we as willing to repay any kind of offenses we have caused by sin? Will we seek to restore a man's reputation that was destroyed by our gossip? Have you ever cheated a bit on your income tax return? Would you send four times that amount to the IRS?

Zacchaeus

Did you tell the car dealer all that was wrong with that car you traded in? Did you list all the flaws in the house you sold? Have you ever fudged on your travel allowance? Have you ever carried some of the company's property home with you—a pencil, paper, a wrench, etc.? Have you ever called in sick when you weren't? Have you ever extended your lunch hour? Ever used the company's phone for personal long-distance calls?

How about it? Could you give back four times? Jesus liked that attitude. He said to Zacchaeus, "Today salvation has come to this house" (19:9). Could Jesus look at our repentance and say, "You have caught on to what I am all about"?

Conclusion

The last people in the world we would consider worthy for the kingdom of God became great followers of Jesus because He showed them He cared. Let us never forget that God loves the rich as well as the poor. We must not be prejudiced against the rich; we must not be reluctant to win them to Christ.

The rich can show us what it means not to be afraid of humiliation, how to be committed, and how to share our material goods with others. Let us show them we care about their future rather than their fortune.

The Lowest
of the Low

She was guilty! She was wrong! And she got caught! We don't know her name, but we know she was a sinner.

She was a Jew, a part of the brotherhood. Now she was with God's people, but she had no fellowship with them. Fingers were pointing to her in disgust, and those fingers belonged to her religious leaders. These leaders sought out a fellow church member in order to trip her up. They *wanted* to catch her in the sinful act, and they did.

These leaders knew their doctrine; they knew every jot and tittle of their religion. They had the truth, but they had no mercy or grace. Instead of seeing the woman as a sister to help, they saw her as a sinner to kick. They exposed her in public, shouting, "Look what she has done. Look how bad she is! This is why she has not been coming to the assembly. She is no good. She is not worth the effort to save. She will taint us all." And all this happened in the area that was set aside for the worship of God (John 8:2-11)!

There is a great danger that lurks in being knowledgeable in the letter of the law, for one easily can become a heresy-hunter. It is one thing to look for flaws and correct them. It is another matter to look at the lives of others, trying and hoping to find an irregularity so we can point the fingers of judge, jury, and executor. The more we know our doctrine, the higher our position of leadership in the church, the more prevalent this danger becomes. Heresy-hunting to such an extreme is one of the major tools used by the devil to spread discord within the church of God.

Here was a woman in need. The church should be the one place where the guilty can come and feel welcomed and understood. Sinners should be forgiven and allowed to fellowship with the church people. Sin is a barrier between people, but church people should seek to tear down that barrier and enter to touch a sister, rather than taunt a sinner.

It was an ugly scene, but Jesus stooped down to write on the ground. Stooping was a position of shame in that day. I suspect He was ashamed of their heartless reaction toward her. Then He spoke. He spoke to the circle of pointing fingers. "I am the only one who can condemn her. You have no right to pick up stones and throw them at her, whether the stones are rocks or words. You have no right to pick them up and aim

them toward another's destruction, for every one of you has also sinned."*

Then Jesus turned to the woman in the circle of accusation and stood in the middle with her in silence. The condemning fingers disappeared as the accusers walked away one by one. The scene then became a beautiful one. The sinner stood with the Sinless, and the fetters of men were replaced with the forgiveness of a gracious Master.

We do not know if her life changed or if she grew to be like Jesus. She is nameless. But we do know what Jesus said to her, "Neither do I condemn you; go your way; from now on sin no more" (v. 11).

How much more beautiful the picture would have been if the church leaders had gone out to find that sister, not to condemn her but to counsel her, not to denounce her but to deliver her from the sin. Then they would bring her to the temple, not to bind her in fetters of the law, but to offer her renewed fellowship of love.

Of which picture would you have been a part? Mature Christians are merciful and forgiving, remembering that they themselves are chief sinners.

Another Nameless One

Jesus was having dinner in the house of some religious leaders. He was reclining at the dinner table with His feet stretched out, when "she" came in uninvited. She knew she was a sinner, and she knew that Jesus could help her. Her heart was wretched at approaching Him in this setting. Yet her faith gave her the courage.

The host, Simon, had not provided a basin of water for Jesus to bathe His feet. This was a common courtesy afforded a traveler, since most people traveled on foot. Sinner or not, the woman must have known the custom. "He must be miserable," she thought. "He's walked so far, and they didn't even give Him water for His feet."

Tears filled her eyes and overflowed onto Jesus' feet. Having no cloth, she wiped them dry with her hair. She then kissed them, an act showing the deepest kind of respect. Then she poured a costly vial of perfume over His feet to refresh and cool them.

Her action caused quite a stir. The Pharisee was enraged at Jesus and at the woman. "If this man were a prophet He would know who and what sort of person this woman is who is touching Him, that she is a sinner," he thought (Luke 7:39).

Yes, she was a sinner. That was how she was introduced to us (v. 37), literally "a woman who by her nature was a sinner in the city." Any Jew touched by a "sinner" would consider himself unclean. Simon knew this, and He also knew that a "true prophet" need not be reminded of it. Certainly a prophet would not allow such touching and kissing by a sinful woman!

But Jesus made it clear that this woman's actions

were superior to those of Simon, His host. "Do you see this woman?" Jesus asked Simon (7:44). That was the problem. Simon did not see *her;* he saw only her sin. He had dismissed her as an unclean thing. We are not much different from Simon sometimes. We look at certain people and see only scum, and that is all we expect them to ever be.

Jesus continued, "She did for me what you would not. She cared for my needs, and she showed respect for me, when you did not" (7:44, 45)*.

Just knowing facts and going through rituals at the correct time (as the Pharisees did) do not exhaust our responsibility to God. Let us remember this woman. She cared for Him.

How do we care for Him today? How do we show respect for Him? Not just by knowing doctrine, attending worship, and working in the church, but also by caring for people who need our care (Matthew 25:31-46). We show respect for Christ by obeying His Word, loving Him and believing in Him, but He also taught us to forgive, show mercy, and to care for one another. (Study Matthew 5:7; 9:13; 18:33.)

Although these women were nameless, they had some great lessons to teach us.

CONCLUSION

What a heavenly Father we have! Although He calls us to be a part of the same family by the same Lord through the same baptism and in the same Spirit, He allows us to retain our differences in personality and aptitudes.

God did not expect Andrew to become exactly like Peter, or Peter to become like Timothy. The church, which is the body of Christ, is made up of many different kinds of members, but it still remains one (1 Corinthians 12:12-17).

God does not expect you to look for someone

else to copy. Don't feel inferior because you are not like some of these people in the book, and don't feel smug because you think you are like all of them.

You are you. Simply thank God for the unique person you are, and then take that uniqueness and aim it toward becoming like Jesus in purpose and character.

Although each person studied in this book was different from the others, in some ways they were all alike. They all had enough trust in Jesus to take His words seriously, and all had the desire to grow beyond the infant stage of Christianity.

We cannot have the same personalities they had, but we can manifest some of the same attitudes. We can become humble and submissive as Mary. We can point others to Jesus, as John the Baptist did. We can be willing to change from a life of selfishness to a life of service as James and John. We can work without credit as Andrew. We can grow out of racial prejudices as Peter. We can encourage others as Barnabas. We can strive to imitate Christ as Paul. We can become bold witnesses, as Ananias and Stephen. We can be peacemakers, as Timothy. We can influence others, as Lois and Eunice. We can work for Christ no matter where we live, as Aquila and Priscilla. We can choose the Master over materialism, as Matthew and Zacchaeus. We can accept forgiveness and show respect, as the two lowly, unnamed women.

If we are making progress in these areas, we are on the way and aiming toward the target. It is quite a challenge to grow up, huh, Christian?